Sustainable Value Creation

The framework presented in this book, *Sustainable Value Creation*, is the result of more than twenty years thinking and writing at the intersection of two subjects, *strategy* and *CSR*. I teach strategy and I think about CSR, almost constantly. Given my academic home in the business school, I appreciate the importance of markets and the ability of their essential actors (for-profit firms) to create value. Equally, of course, I see the ability of firms to destroy value, on an all-too-frequent basis. As such, I have spent a lot of time thinking about how to promote the beneficial work firms do and eradicate the harm. The result is this book: a framework through which managers can understand the essential purpose of the for-profit firm, the most powerful entity we have devised to drive societal progress.

At its core, this book is structured around the ten principles that define *Sustainable Value Creation*. The foundation for these principles is a pragmatic philosophy, oriented around stakeholder theory and designed to appeal to managers skeptical of existing definitions of CSR, sustainability, or business ethics. It is also designed to stimulate thought within the community of academics committed to these ideas, but who approach them from more traditional perspectives. Ultimately, therefore, this book aims to reform both business practice and business education. By building a theory that redefines CSR as central to everything the firm does (as opposed to peripheral practices that can be marginalized), these ten principles redefine how firms approach each of their operational functions, but also how these subjects should be taught in universities worldwide. As such, this book will hopefully be of value to instructors as a complement to their teaching, students as a guide in their education, and managers as a framework to help them respond to the complex, dynamic context that they are expected to navigate every day.

David Chandler is Associate Professor of Management at the University of Colorado Denver Business School. His research focuses on the dynamic interface between the firm and its institutional environment and has been published widely. Additional related publications include the textbook *Strategic Corporate Social Responsibility: Sustainable Value Creation* (5th edition, 2020).

Sustainable Value Creation

Second edition

David Chandler

Routledge
Taylor & Francis Group

LONDON AND NEW YORK

Second edition published 2021
by Routledge
2 Park Square, Milton Park, Abingdon, Oxon, OX14 4RN

and by Routledge
52 Vanderbilt Avenue, New York, NY 10017

Routledge is an imprint of the Taylor & Francis Group, an informa business

[First edition published by Business Expert Press 2015]

British Library Cataloguing-in-Publication Data
A catalogue record for this book is available from the British Library

Library of Congress Cataloging-in-Publication Data
Names: Chandler, David, 1969– author.
Title: Sustainable value creation / David Chandler.
Description: Abingdon, Oxon ; New York, NY : Routledge, 2020. |
Includes bibliographical references and index. | Identifiers: LCCN
2020003901 (print) | LCCN 2020003902 (ebook) | ISBN
9780367859817 (hardback) | ISBN 9780367859824 (paperback) |
ISBN 9781003016199 (ebook)
Subjects: LCSH: Social responsibility of business. | Value.
Classification: LCC HD60 .C4428 2020 (print) | LCC HD60 (ebook)
| DDC 658.4/08–dc23
LC record available at https://lccn.loc.gov/2020003901
LC ebook record available at https://lccn.loc.gov/2020003902

ISBN: 978-0-367-85981-7 (hbk)
ISBN: 978-0-367-85982-4 (pbk)
ISBN: 978-1-003-01619-9 (ebk)

Typeset in Bembo
by Wearset Ltd, Boldon, Tyne and Wear

Visit the eResources: www.routledge.com/9780367859817

Few trends could so thoroughly undermine the very foundations of our free society as the acceptance by corporate officials of a social responsibility other than to make as much money for their stockholders as possible. This is a fundamentally subversive doctrine.

Milton Friedman (1962)[1]

Contents

Foreword

June, 2014[1]

What is the purpose of a business corporation? For much of the past three decades, observers and even many business leaders embraced the view that corporations "belong" to their shareholders and that the legal responsibility of corporate directors and executives is to single-mindedly seek to maximize shareholder wealth. Today, experts and laypersons alike increasingly recognize this view of business to be both mistaken and harmful.

As a purely factual matter, corporate law does not require directors and executives to try and maximize profits or share price. Although a business must be profitable to survive, corporate law grants executives and directors of business corporations the discretion to pursue any lawful purpose as a business goal. This "business judgment rule" is something that is consistent across almost all legal jurisdictions.

Nor do shareholders own corporations. Corporations, as legal entities, own themselves. Shareholders own shares that are legal contracts with the corporate entity, just as employees own employment contracts with the entity and bondholders own debt contracts with the corporate entity. A firm's shareholder body is an important partner, but only one of many.

The combined effect of these legal realities, which are the products of decades of both case and statutory law, is to liberate executives and directors to pursue a wide range of practices that they believe to be in the best interests of the organization as a whole. In other words, executives and directors are not bound by any imperative to maximize profits for shareholders in the short term, but can seek to sustain the organization over the medium and long term, ensuring that value is created for a broad range of constituents.

This is important because, from a practical perspective, the dogma of "maximizing shareholder value" does not seem to be working out particularly well for the companies that choose to adopt it. In the quest to "unlock shareholder value," managers have sold off key assets; fired valuable employees; leveraged firms to the brink of bankruptcy; and showered CEOs with stock options in order to "incentivize" them to raise the share price. Some have even committed fraud. Such strategies have proved harmful not only to customers, employees, and taxpayers, but to shareholders themselves. Indeed, even as the business sector has embraced the ideology of shareholder value, shareholder returns from holding public equity have declined. Society, as a whole, is worse off as a result.

This book helps explain why. The framework detailed by David Chandler offers a roadmap for building companies that can do more not only for shareholders, but also for customers, suppliers, employees, and society as a whole. The questions *Who owns the firm?* and *In whose interests should the firm be run?* are central to this quest. Once we successfully challenge the idea that shareholders own the firm, we remove much of the pressure that drives executives and directors to always favor shareholders' interests over the interests of other stakeholders who are often more invested in the organization and more central to its sustained success.

Corporate Social Responsibility: A Strategic Perspective offers compelling arguments against shareholder primacy. In its place, it presents an alternative vision of *strategic CSR* that builds on a foundation of stakeholder theory and takes into account core insights from the fields of psychology and economics to demonstrate that it is in the strategic interests of the firm to respond to the values, needs, and concerns of all stakeholders. Through this approach, firms generate the most value for the broadest section of society.

Corporate Social Responsibility: A Strategic Perspective is a manifesto for business today. It is essential reading for academics interested in CSR, for students interested in business, and for executives who seek insight into the complex web of competing stakeholder interests they must balance every day.

Lynn A. Stout
Distinguished Professor of Corporate and Business Law
Jack G. Clarke Business Law Institute, Cornell Law School

Acknowledgments

The framework presented in this book, *Sustainable Value Creation*, is the result of more than 20 years' thinking and writing at the intersection of two subjects, *strategy* and *CSR*. I teach strategy and I think about CSR, almost constantly. Given my academic home in the business school, I appreciate the importance of markets and the ability of their essential actors (for-profit firms) to create value. Equally, of course, I see the ability of firms to destroy value, on an all-too-frequent basis. As such, I have spent a lot of time thinking about how to promote the beneficial work firms do and eradicate the harm. The result is this book – a framework through which managers can understand the essential purpose of the for-profit firm, the most powerful entity we have devised to drive societal progress.

This framework, as far as I can see from the constant stream of CSR-related articles that cross my desk, is unique. I also believe it is revolutionary. It challenges much of what is currently taken-for-granted about CSR, both as it is taught in universities and practiced in corporations. The consequences of this contrary approach can be seen in answer to the essential question, *What does it mean for a firm to be socially responsible?* If you ask that question in most CSR classes, I believe the answer would be that it looks something like Patagonia or TOMS; with *SVC*, it is Walmart (or Amazon or Apple). If you ask that question in most corporations, I believe the answer would be that it looks something like philanthropy or employee volunteer programs; with *SVC*, it is strategy and core operations. Understanding why these differences are so stark will alter your understanding of business – what the firm *is* and what it *does*.

When I began this journey in the mid-1990s, I held a more traditional CSR perspective. It has taken me over 20 years of reading, about economics and social psychology, to reject what I previously accepted. But, although this perspective is mine and is something for which I am solely accountable, I was only able to develop it with considerable help along the way. In particular, when I think about the intersection of strategy and CSR, I think about the intersection of two Bills: First, Bill Werther, who taught me much of what I needed to know about *strategy* and how to be an academic; and second, the late Bill Frederick, whose intellectual depth and generosity continue to shape the fields of *CSR* and *business ethics* and will do so for many generations of academics to come. I owe a great deal to both Bills.

More specifically, this book benefitted from the insights and constructive criticism of many friends and colleagues as the core ideas were being developed. In particular for the first edition, the following people kindly gave their time and attention to read early drafts and provide feedback: Bart Alexander of Alexander & Associates, LLC; Michael L. Barnett of Rutgers University; Mark A. Buchanan of Boise State University; William C. Frederick of the University of Pittsburgh (emeritus); R. Edward Freeman of the University of Virginia; Stuart L. Hart of the University of Vermont; Laura Pincus Hartman of DePaul University; Joshua D. Margolis of Harvard University; Miguel Athayde Marques of Católica University; James E. Post of Boston University (emeritus); Mark P. Sharfman of the University of Oklahoma; Lynn A. Stout of Cornell University; Roy Suddaby of the University of Victoria; and William B. Werther of the University of Miami. While all errors are mine, this book is significantly better due to their expertise.

I am also indebted to a number of colleagues who kindly agreed to review the proposal (both named and anonymously) for this edition of the book, including: Robert Arp of Webster University; Kevin Eckerle of New York University; Scott Freehafer of the University of Findlay; Bruce Kibler of Gannon University; Seoki Lee of Pennsylvania State University; Karen Palumbo of the University of Saint Francis; and Andrew Trew of John Carroll University. The constructive feedback of these experienced teachers, drawn from many years of experience in the classroom, ensured that this edition of *SVC* is considerably better than it otherwise would have been.

Finally, I would like to thank the editorial team at Routledge for their assistance in preparing this manuscript. In particular, I would like to thank the senior editor who commissioned this edition of the book, Rebecca Marsh. Rebecca is a big reason why I decided to revisit this framework, and I am very happy she persuaded me to do so. More broadly, it is the support of publishers like Routledge for projects like this that help realize the goal of building a stronger intellectual framework for more responsible management education practices in universities around the world.

Introduction

Corporate Social Responsibility

Corporate Social Responsibility (CSR), on the surface, is flourishing. In its various guises, CSR appears to be everywhere as firms rush to respond to the ever-evolving and seemingly never-ending demands of their stakeholders. In whatever direction CEOs turn, they are being pressed for an opinion about this controversial topic, or asked to take action to introduce that progressive change. Everything they say and do is fraught with danger as they try to navigate what, to many, is new terrain. The moment feels different, and CSR appears to be driving both the uncertainty and the excitement that accompanies it.

As a movement for meaningful change, however, there is a more convincing argument that says CSR is floundering. We have yet to agree on a single definition, we do not know how to measure it, and we have failed to make a compelling business case for it. Most firms equate CSR with peripheral activities, such as philanthropy or employee volunteer programs, while short-term shareholder primacy continues to dominate the business landscape.[1] This, in spite of revisions of the purpose of the firm promoting stakeholder capitalism announced by both the Business Roundtable[2] and the World Economic Forum.[3] If radical change was the goal, then 70 years of CSR has failed.[4] The economy today is no more sustainable than it ever was, while emissions of carbon dioxide and other greenhouse gasses sit at "a record high."[5]

Given the stakes, an alternative approach is required. The response advocated in this book is *Sustainable Value Creation (SVC)* – a reinterpretation of the relationships firms have with their broad range of stakeholders that are fundamental to the value creating purpose of the for-profit firm in a capitalist society. In particular, this book presents the ten defining principles of *SVC*. Together, they constitute a critique of the current CSR discussion, while building a framework that can be integrated into the firm's strategic planning process and across operations. As such, *SVC* is in the firm's best interest; it also produces optimal outcomes for society.

At its core, this book makes the following case: If the purpose of a firm's strategy is to build a sustainable competitive advantage that can be sustained over the medium to long term, then the best way to do that in today's complex, dynamic business environment is to create value for the firm's stakeholders, broadly defined. While the firm cannot please all of its stake-holders all of the time, the firm's job (and, in particular, that of the firm's man-agers) should be to please as many stakeholders as much of the time as possible. While this may sound straightforward, however, it is incredibly difficult in practice. It is what makes management such a challenge because competing claims are constantly being made on a finite set of available resources. Worse, the manager must not only understand what the firm's stakeholders want today, but be able to predict what they are going to want tomorrow.

In order to tackle their task, the manager first has to understand the basics of economic exchange (how firms operate, what profit represents, etc.) and then, equally important, social psychology (how humans make decisions, react to incentives, define value, etc.). In other words, if you want to under-stand macro-level market dynamics, you need economics; while, if you want to understand micro-level human decision-making, you need (social) psych-ology. To understand *business*, you need both. That is the purpose of this book – to incorporate what we know about economic theory and human psychology to explain how a complex social system (i.e., a market-based economy) functions. In the process, this book challenges many of the taken-for-granted assumptions of the CSR debate. In their place, it builds a frame-work for stakeholder value creation that exists at the center of the firm's purpose – *Sustainable Value Creation*.

An essential step in this process, therefore, is to redefine what we mean by CSR. For too long, CSR has been relegated to the periphery of operations. As a result, it has been marginalized as an organizing principle of the firm, as Milton Friedman's quote on the dedication page of this book suggests. Fried-man dismissed CSR as "a fundamentally subversive doctrine"[6] because he saw it as a harmful distraction; a waste of the firm's time and effort – or, as he might have put it, the inefficient allocation of scarce and valuable resources. Advocates of CSR have done little to alter this perception in the decades since, which has allowed critics to continue to dismiss CSR as secondary to what the firm is and does. In contrast, *SVC* redefines CSR as central to the firm's identity and oper-ations. All firms have stakeholders and all firms, to varying degrees, create value for those stakeholders. Everything the firm does contributes to this process. Seen in this light, business and *SVC* (or CSR, redefined) are synonymous. But we are getting ahead of ourselves. Before we can arrive at this conclusion, it is important to understand why this redefinition is necessary – in short, we need to know what is currently wrong with CSR.

Defining CSR

What is *Corporate Social Responsibility* (CSR)? What is *sustainability*? What is the difference between these two concepts and *business ethics*? Is CR (*Corpo-rate Responsibility*) different from CSR? Is a firm's *purpose* different from its *responsibility*? What does it mean to be a *corporate citizen*? All of these terms have become commonplace in recent years, but beyond a general sense that corporations have some form of obligation beyond their organizational boundaries, what do they actually mean? Are these concepts mutually exclusive or is there significant overlap among them? And, if they are not the same, why is it that we cannot agree upon universal definitions that convey clearly to firms the set of behaviors expected of them?[7]

> Right now we're in a free-for-all in which "CSR" means whatever a company wants it to mean: From sending employees out in matching t-shirts to paint a wall for five hours a year, to recycling, to improving supply-chain conditions, to diversity and inclusion. This makes it difficult to have a proper conversation about what corporate responsibilities are and should be.[8]

In other words, in spite of a large and growing amount of work that seeks to understand a firm's *social responsibility*, there remains great confusion and inconsistency. Far from the absence of possible definitions, however, as the above list of terms suggests, "the problem is rather that there is an abundance of definitions, which are ... often biased toward specific interests and thus prevent the development and implementations of the concept."[9] As a result, while there is broad agreement about the idea that firms have a social responsibility, there is little agreement on what that responsibility looks like in practice:

> There is ... considerable debate as to whether [society] requires more of the corporation than the obvious: ... creating and delivering products and services consumers want, providing employment and career opportunities for employees, developing markets for suppliers, and paying taxes to governments and returns to shareholders and other claimants on the rents generated by the corporation.[10]

How can we argue that CSR is important if we cannot agree what CSR is, or at least narrow it down to a reasonable set of definitions?[11] If CSR remains idiosyncratic (different things to different people), then it loses its essential meaning and ability to influence the way we structure the economic order. This confusion suggests the need for additional clarification, and hopefully some agreement, in terms of what we mean when we talk about *CSR*.

Measuring CSR

Central to the challenge of defining CSR is the ability to measure CSR. You have to know what something is before you can quantify it; equally, you have to be able to measure it before it can be widely disseminated. Unfortunately, because we have not been able to define CSR, we have also not done a very good job of measuring CSR. And, as a direct result, we cannot easily say which firms are better or worse at CSR (as an objective fact). Even more problematic, although we have some intuitive sense of which firms are *good* and which firms are *bad* (based on our individual assumptions and values), we are presently unable to compare one firm to another reliably across all aspects of operations (particularly if the firms operate in different industries). The reason we are not able to do these things, of course, is because they are incredibly difficult. It is certainly not for want of trying. But the challenges involved in defining societal expectations and then quantifying those expectations holistically in terms of firm performance quickly become apparent with a simple thought experiment. Consider the complexities inherent in any attempt to parcel out and quantify the impact an individual firm's operations has on the environment:

> Let's suppose changes in average world temperature lead to the extinction of, let's say Blue Whales, and an obscure currently undiscovered insect in the Amazon. What valuation would we place on the Blue Whale, and how would we calculate it? On the potential economic value of products that might be extracted from it? On the basis of what someone would be prepared to pay for its existence to be preserved? And what about the insect we never even heard of? Suppose it might hold the secret of a new pharmaceutical discovery? Or then again, it might not.[12]

While we may be able to agree that the aggregate effect of all economic activity is detrimental and causing climate change,[13] the degree to which it is doing so and what we might do about it remains unclear. In essence, calculating the present–day value of that future cost and determining what percentage can be attributed to an individual firm is extremely challenging. Should a firm be responsible only for the costs incurred during the production of its products, for example, or also for those incurred during their consumption? Should automobile companies be held responsible for the pollution caused by people driving cars or only for the pollution involved in making the cars? What about smartphone companies, where there is little cost to the environment during consumption of the product, but the potential for significant damage during disposal due to e-waste? And, what about a firm's supply chain – where does one firm's responsibility begin and another's end? Should a sports shoe company be responsible for the costs incurred during the manufacture of the shoe (even though that process is completed by an independent contractor)? What about any work that is further outsourced by that contractor to a sub-contractor? What about the rubber used to make the soles of the shoes – is that also the sports shoe company's responsibility, or the responsibility of the contractor (or sub-contractor) who purchased the raw material, or of the plantation where the rubber was initially harvested? There are no easy answers to these questions, which relate only to the *costs* incurred by a firm. What about quantifying the *benefits* the firm and its products provide, which raise a whole new set of challenges? And, perhaps most importantly, how should these benefits offset the costs – should we sum them to create a net effect or should the costs be weighted more heavily than the benefits (or vice-versa)?

In spite of these complexities (and many more), the idea that firms have a *social responsibility* continues to capture our attention.[14] We remain convinced that this special thing we are talking about, CSR, matters. It must matter, right? After all, being *responsible* has to be better than being *irresponsible*. And it is important for our sense of justice that those firms that are more responsible should be rewarded in some way, while those firms that are less responsible should be punished. But, what if the reverse is true and it is those firms that make the most effort to be socially responsible that are penalized for doing so by stakeholders who fail to reward the behavior they claim to want from firms (and fail to punish the behavior they say they do not want)?[15] Ultimately, if we cannot develop consistent definitions of good/bad, better/worse, and then construct a set of measures that capture the extent to which these ideas are implemented in practice, how can we determine whether CSR actually matters?

> The empirical literature on the relationship between CSR and performance is mixed and fraught with empirical question marks around not just how performance is measured but what it means to "do good." … we simply do not understand the causal link between a firm's specific CSR activities and the operational outcomes that can influence performance.[16]

We need to get this right because erroneous assumptions and inconsistent empirical correlations cause deterministic judgments to be made about these essential ideas. If we are honest with ourselves, we would understand that, in spite of large numbers of studies on this topic[17] and the tireless work of groups such as SASB, CDP, and GRI,[18] we do not yet have the capability to measure the all-encompassing nature of CSR. On the contrary, there is good reason to believe that not only are we unable to measure CSR, but that the measures we have are gravely misleading. That would explain why firms like Enron and BP can win CSR, sustainability, and business ethics awards shortly before they commit devastating ethics and environmental transgressions. It also explains why it has been reported that there is "total chaos" surrounding ESG[19] reporting in the U.S.,[20] with few established standards resulting in "the current hotchpotch of competing (and often misleading) measures of how firms fare."[21] As one analyst reported:

> In one year, a large industrial company was recognized as a top 10 ESG performer by one data provider and a bottom 10 ESG performer by another. … Both [monitors] had legitimate considerations, [which suggests] large public companies are complex and dynamic in a way that does not lend itself to absolutism.[22]

One reason for this confusion is that different monitoring firms place different weights on the different ESG dimensions. Even the philosophical question, "Should a highly polluting company be able to offset that [pollution] by having great governance and treating workers well?" is challenging.[23] The result, of course, is different results for the same firm, depending on the priorities (and biases) of the organization conducting the evaluation. Comparing Exxon's ESG score against four firms in different industries, for example:

> Sustainalytics ranks Exxon top of the five companies overall because it puts a 40% weight on social issues, where Exxon does well thanks to strong policies for its workers, supply chain and local communities. MSCI ranks Exxon fourth of the five in part because it puts a 51% weight on environment and only 17% on social issues.[24]

In spite of the apparent futility involved in measuring a firm's CSR profile, does that mean we have to throw up our hands and surrender, relying instead on subjective moral and ethical arguments designed to persuade managers to *do the right thing*? To the extent that we can arrive at a standardized way of measuring what we agree should be measured, then we will be able to compare one firm's activity with another's.[25] Whether those numbers are 100% accurate is less important than whether any biases are known and applied equally across all firms. So many of our measurements involve subjective interpretations and assumptions, but are widely perceived as objective statements of fact (e.g., think about how accountants measure brand value or goodwill). Placing a cost on the extinction of the Blue Whale versus the lost opportunity of an unrealized pharmaceutical discovery will always involve some element of subjectivity and debate. Nevertheless, there is a great deal of benefit in being able to construct a relative and standardized measure of which firms add more or less value. Doing so will help us define CSR accurately and in a way that encourages the reforms in our corporations that are essential to building a more sustainable, value-adding economic system.

This pursuit of defining and measuring CSR is essential because the question *What is the purpose of the for-profit firm in society?* is highly consequential. Whether we are talking about environmental degradation or social cohesion, wealth distribution or global free trade, the answer to this question defines our immediate and future quality of existence. It determines the society we live in and will pass on to future generations. While some people argue it is impossible to conclude whether a firm is truly socially responsible,[26] the more essential question is relative (rather than absolute). In other words, it is important to identify those firms that are more or less responsible than others, without needing to make definitive claims as to whether a firm is objectively responsible or irresponsible. While recognizing the challenges in doing so, being able to identify the business models that create more value is a challenge that seems to be inherently worth tackling. Yet, the confusion sown by inconsistent definitions, partial measures, and the multitude of labels and rating systems that purport to reveal which products and which firms are *green, ethical,* or *socially responsible* serves only to undermine the good intentions of all involved.

Urgently, we need to agree on a definition of CSR and recognize that, until we can measure this complex construct, we should be careful about drawing definitive conclusions based on unrepresentative empirical studies. Rather than rely on good intentions, which inevitably lead us to inaccurate conclusions, perhaps a more constructive approach would be to turn to economic fundamentals, which have been measuring societal impact for centuries.

Profiting from CSR

If we are able to agree on a definition of CSR and then begin to measure this elusive concept, we would be in a much better position to answer the question: *What is the business case for CSR?* The challenge in answering this question is related directly to our inability to agree on what we want firms to do and to know whether they are actually doing it. Conceptually, the collective failure of advocates to construct a convincing argument in favor of CSR also reflects a fundamental debate that is yet to be resolved – whether CSR should be voluntary or mandatory.

In the absence of a compelling argument built around self-interest, most of the debate about CSR seeks to compel firms to act more responsibly. Whether via moral or ethical guilt, normative association, or restrictive legislation, many advocates believe CSR should be coerced, rather than incentivized. This perspective is founded on the assumption that managers do not believe CSR to be in the best interests of the firm (and, by extension, themselves) and that, as a result, they are either unable or unwilling to act in ways that benefit society unless compelled to do so.

This book rejects that assumption on two levels. First, the argument that is framed here is based on the idea that it is only firms that incorporate CSR voluntarily into their strategic planning and all aspects of operations that will do so comprehensively and genuinely. And second that, as a result, building this argument around enlightened self-interest is our best hope of introducing meaningful change. Comprehensive and genuine implementation is likely to generate further innovation and creativity (and social benefit), while selective and coerced implementation is likely to result in resistance and obstruction (and social harm). Worse, by compelling CSR, the danger is that it becomes something to be avoided, rather than something to be embraced – an *obligation* rather than an *opportunity*.[27] The course of human development demonstrates the fallibility of coercion, while the progress our society has made since the industrial revolution reveals the powerful benefits that spring from the pursuit of self-interest. In *free* societies, humans (and, by extension, organizations) are effective at avoiding coercion – we resist efforts to control and constrain our collective productivity:

> the soundest objection to government intervention in business is not that the matter is none of the government's affair, for it is everybody's affair; the essential point is that controls imposed from without are always less authentic in a dynamic sense than those evolved from within.[28]

For-profit firms are most efficient when they are acting in their own self-interest. The most effective laws are those that are founded on widespread social support. If such support is widespread, however, then that behavior is generally accepted as normative (and the law is therefore less necessary). Over-zealous attempts to constrain market forces, on the other hand, will generate unintended consequences as firms seek to evade artificial limits. As noted by *The Economist*, "Finance has yet to meet a rule it doesn't want to game," while, in general, "[capital flows] to where frictions are lowest."[29] If the intended target does not agree with a specific law or regulation, it will attempt to subvert it, however surreptitiously. In fact, such behavior will often be encouraged by that very same law or regulation that is, by definition, broad and ambiguous because it is intended to apply so widely. There is a reason why, for example, corporations employ armies of skilled accountants whose job is to find ways for the organization to avoid paying taxes:

> The United States income tax laws allow companies to claim they earned profits in countries where they actually had few, if any, operations, but where taxes are extremely low. ... the U.S. Public Interest Research Group Education Fund and Citizens for Tax Justice, said that 372 of the companies in the Fortune 500 ... reported a total of 7,827 subsidiaries in countries that the groups view as tax havens. Some of those subsidiaries no doubt do real business. ... But most ... are engaged only in the business of tax avoidance.[30]

Whether such behavior is *right* or *ideal* is a complicated discussion that revolves around the roots of human innovation and creativity. Nevertheless, it is central to the framework presented here that any attempt to amend capitalism in a way that encourages more socially beneficial behavior will be most effective when it is aligned with firms' self-interest, which is related directly to economic success. While we can argue that any particular policy is more or less beneficial, it is the contention of this book that we will only succeed in developing a holistic *business case* when firms integrate CSR fully throughout operations and create an environment in which it is understood to be in their best interest to do so.

To date, a sufficiently convincing case has not been made to managers that CSR is of strategic value to the firm. The lack of specificity in terms of both defining and measuring CSR suggests the need for a new conceptualization that is grounded in a business-focused perspective – one that is pragmatic, rather than idealistic; one that deals with human nature as we know it to be, rather than as we may wish it were.[31]

Sustainable Value Creation

Together, our failure to adequately define CSR, measure CSR, and build the business case for CSR suggests the need for an alternative approach.

The response advocated in this book is a framework grounded in empirical observation and developed over more than two decades of thinking and writing about CSR – *SVC*.[32] Specifically, this book establishes a set of unifying principles that define the intellectual debate around CSR, while also providing a program for managers to implement what, up until now, has been a collection of interesting ideals, but has fallen short of a coherent philosophy and plan of action.

As discussed above, "After more than half a century of research and debate, there is not a single widely accepted definition of CSR."[33] Importantly, however, although there is no commonly agreed definition, it is acknowledged that there has been a common purpose to all of the work produced in the name of CSR – "to broaden the obligations of firms to include more than financial considerations."[34] The field of CSR and business ethics has long focused on the ends of business – forcing firms to focus on goals other than, or in addition to, profit. The result has been a lot of wasted energy and a large number of premature pronouncements. As Howard Bowen claimed optimistically in his foundational 1953 book, the *Social Responsibilities of the Businessman*:

> The day of plunder, human exploitation, and financial chicanery by private businessmen [sic] has largely passed. And the day when profit maximization was the sole criterion of business success is rapidly fading. We are entering an era when private business will be judged solely in terms of its demonstrable contribution to the general welfare.[35]

Urging firms to "include more than financial considerations" as part of their business model is not the purpose of this book and, in my use of the term, it is also not the purpose of *SVC*. The goal of this book is to refocus the CSR debate onto the *means* of business, rather than the *ends*. Demanding that managers expand the goals of the firm suggests a problem with the ends of capitalism (i.e., profit). In contrast, the underlying principles of *SVC* suggest that any problem with capitalism, as currently practiced, is not with the ends but the means. Seeking profit (which is the best measure we have of long-term value-added) is not the problem; it is the methods by which profit is sought that can be problematic. In other words, it is not what firms do, but how they do it that matters. When rules are broken, costs are externalized, and key stakeholders ignored (or worse, abused), value is broadly diminished. While some firms may benefit from such practices in the short term, such antagonistic behavior that benefits only a narrow subset of constituents is difficult to sustain. Meanwhile, the costs are borne by society as a whole.[36]

Put another way, it is the environment in which the firm operates that creates the boundary conditions that define what the pursuit of profit means at any given point. The *rules of the game* determine what is acceptable and unacceptable in the way that any single firm conducts operations. The goal (profit) stays the same and has always been so, back to the earliest markets on the Silk Road; it is the rules that evolve and vary from culture to culture. And, it is the more astute managers who understand the current conditions and when the rules (both written and unwritten) have shifted who can guide their firms to greater economic success. They understand that abiding by those rules provides the firm with the license it requires to operate.[37] But, for this relationship to work, it is essential that the rules are enforced. If the rules are enforced, they will determine the outcome.

The business case for CSR, therefore, originates within the firm. It is a process by which managers interpret the shifting environment in a way that allows their firm to be successful. In other words, it is in the firm's self-interest to understand the rules as they are constructed by their stakeholders (internal and external) and abide by them. The problem, of course, is that there is no rule book, per se, and the signals that the firm receives on a day-to-day basis are not consistent, but are many, varied, and contradictory. There is a limited market for sweatshop-free T-shirts, for example, but great savings to be made in waste reduction. Similarly, consumers have demonstrated limited loyalties to firms with a reputation for CSR, but employees are more likely to want to work for such firms. If key stakeholders react positively to a new practice, then it becomes in the self-interest of the firm to continue with that practice. Equally, if key stakeholders disengage or punish the firm for the same action, then the firm would be foolish to continue doing it.

The key is that the motivation to act must be internally generated, based on an iterative relationship with all the different components of society (business and non-business) that create the rules that constitute the social fabric. Laws are one way that these rules are defined for firms (the government is a stakeholder), but only one of many and, as argued above and throughout this book, one of the least efficient. More effective are the myriad signals that customers, employees, suppliers, non-governmental organizations (NGOs), the media, and any other invested constituent conveys to the firm through their day-to-day interactions with it. The result is complex and the message is often garbled, but the stakes for everyone involved are high.

It is not necessarily the case that firms that ignore these rules will immediately fail but, instead, that they will gradually find their degrees of freedom to operate increasingly constricted. In this sense, therefore, much of what is meant by CSR can be captured in a progressive approach to management. As new rules are formed and societal expectations coalesce around these new standards, those firms that understand and abide by them (and anticipate future evolutions) will find the conditions under which they seek profit are easier than those firms that resist. That is what CEOs are experiencing today when they are asked to take a stand on same-sex partner benefits, or the current political administration, or religion in the workplace, or any number of other controversial social issues that increasingly demand their attention. This book is designed to detail the principles on which these new rules are constantly being redefined for those managers who are sufficiently sensitive to detect them and react.

Plan of the book

If *SVC* is to be widely accepted by the business community, it has to establish itself as a comprehensive approach to business, replete with its own set of assumptions and guiding principles. This will allow *SVC* to be studied as a conceptual framework, but also implemented as a realizable set of practices. Specifically, this book is structured around a set of ten defining principles that define *SVC* and enable it to be integrated into the firm's strategic planning process and across operations. It builds the case that *SVC* is a strategic decision that is in the best interests of the firm and all its stakeholders. Following this Introduction, ten chapters present and discuss each of the principles in turn, followed by a concluding chapter that integrates all ten principles into an overarching discussion of the concept of *SVC*.

The ten defining principles of *SVC*, together, constitute a pragmatic philosophy, extending stakeholder theory and designed to persuade managers skeptical of existing definitions and organizing principles of CSR, sustainability, or business ethics. It is also designed to stimulate thought within the community of academics committed to these ideas, but who approach them from more traditional perspectives – how these ideas are taught is as important as how they are practiced. Most importantly, the goal of this book is to solidify the intellectual framework around an emerging concept, *SVC*, that I believe is essential to our future progress and continued prosperity.

Ultimately, therefore, the purpose of this book is radical. By building a theory that redefines CSR as core to business operations and value creation (as opposed to a set of peripheral practices that can be marginalized), these defining principles become applicable across the range of operational functions. In the process, they redefine how businesses approach each of these functions in practice, but also how these subjects should be taught in universities worldwide. To internalize these ten principles is to understand how the firm can respond to stakeholder needs to optimize value creation over the medium to long term. In short, it is a manifesto for success in business in the twenty-first century.

Principle 1

Business is social progress

Key takeaway: There is a direct correlation between the amount of business in a society and the extent of progress enjoyed by that society. For-profit firms are the most effective means of achieving that progress.

Principle 1 states that business *is* progress. In other words, as a general rule, the more business that exists within a community, the greater the economic and social progress that community will experience. Central to the delivery of that progress is the for-profit firm, which has long been one of the most effective means for humans to channel their innovation and creativity. As Micklethwait and Wooldridge note in their history of the company:

> Today, the number of private-sector companies that a country boasts … is a better guide to its status than the number of battleships it can muster. It is also not a bad guide to its political freedom.[1]

In short, society is stronger when capital flows freely and business is incentivized to innovate and compete. This may seem intuitive when we stop and write it down, but the point is not made often enough. And, in its rush to improve an economic system that has already delivered phenomenal social progress, many in the CSR community overlook this fundamental aspect of capitalism. This does not mean that improvements should not be made and certainly does not mean that the government does not have a role to play, but keeping this starting point in mind anchors the framework underpinning *Sustainable Value Creation* (*SVC*).

For-profit firms

Broadly speaking, there are three types of organizations: for-profit, not-for-profit, and governmental. There are also hybrid mixes of these three forms, such as social businesses, government-backed enterprises, and benefit corporations.[2] Of the basic forms, however, only the for-profit firm is consistently able to combine scarce and valuable resources efficiently and on the scale necessary to improve meaningfully our society and standard of living. This unique position of for-profit firms in our society is enhanced when we consider the challenges we face, the timeframe in which substantive action is required, and the complexity inherent in what the former CEO of Unilever, Paul Polman, calls today's "vuca world; volatile, uncertain, complex and ambiguous."[3]

In general, there are two sides to the debate as to how firms should navigate this dynamic environment. On the one hand, for-profit firms receive much from society that is essential for them to operate – a stable legal system, an educated workforce, a modern infrastructure, and so on. As such, many CSR advocates argue that firms have a broader responsibility to recognize (and appreciate) that they externalize many of the costs that are associated with these benefits. Some of these costs are implicit in the social contract and are a universal good (such as an educated workforce); some of these costs, however, have harmful societal consequences (such as pollution). Either way, firms rely on society to thrive – they "receive a social sanction from society that requires that they, in return, contribute to the growth and development of that society."[4]

On the other hand, however, society receives much from strong, for-profit firms that operate within a vibrant, market-based economy. Look around you. Virtually everything you can see was made by a for-profit firm. It is for-profit firms that are responsible either for much of the innovation that allows society to progress or for converting the innovations made by others (e.g., scientists, artists, and academics) into products that make our lives better. More important than the value added by for-profit organizations through innovation, however, is the efficient means by which they are able to convert valuable and scarce resources into usable products, and distribute those products to those who demand them at the price those individuals are willing to pay. The details of this process (what for-profit firms do and how they do it) defines our quality of life and our level of social progress. The recognition of this leads supporters to claim that:

> The most important organization in the world is the company: the basis of the prosperity of the West and the best hope for the future of the rest of the world.[5]

In other words, while firms benefit greatly from a stable and enlightened society, society also benefits greatly from a vigorous, competitive set of for-profit firms. In considering these tradeoffs and tensions, however, it is important to remind ourselves that juxtaposing firms and society in this way, as many in the CSR community continue to do, suggests that firms and society are independent of each other. In reality, of course, they are inseparable. Firms exist as part of society in the same way that society is made up of many functioning parts, an important component of which is for-profit firms.

Equally, managers, board directors, employees, and shareholders each have additional roles elsewhere in society (as consumers, activists, volunteers, community members, etc.), as well as working together at the same for-profit firm.

In essence, therefore, business and society are interwoven – their interests are aligned and business has as much to gain from a strong and healthy society as society has to lose from a constrained and ineffective business sector. The question, therefore, is not *What do firms owe society?* or *What does society owe firms?* but, instead, is the more nuanced debate about *What role do firms play in society?* While social progress over centuries demonstrates the inescapable value of for-profit firms within a market-based system, each firm should be routinely assessed to determine whether their individual contribution is net positive or net negative. Where it is net positive, we need to ask *Is that contribution as good as it can be?* Alternatively, where it is net negative, we should inquire *How can we introduce incentives to improve performance?* But, each firm's interest lies not in waiting for this evaluation to be imposed externally, but initiating it to ensure its operations meet the ever-shifting expectations placed upon it. Paul Polman understands this iterative dynamic better than most:

> Business simply can't be a bystander in a system that gives it life in the first place. We have to take responsibility, and that requires more long-term thinking about our business model.[6]

Addressing these questions and providing constructive answers, I believe, is the most important challenge our society faces today.

Business is ethical and moral

It is impossible to separate ethics and morals from any aspect of human behavior. Everything we do involves ethical and moral components and, more often than not, tradeoffs among ideals. These same tensions and pressures exist in business. All aspects of a firm's operations, to some degree, have moral, ethical, or value-laden elements.[7] While we may agree or disagree about whether an employee should be paid a living wage or a minimum wage, for example, there is no doubt that the decision is consequential for the firm, the employee, and for the society in which both exist. As a result, there is an ethical and moral perspective from which the problem can be addressed, and about which we can agree or disagree. These same considerations and conflicts extend to all aspects of operations:

> When a businessman decides whether or not to produce a new product or service, he is helping to decide the range of products available to customers. When he decides whether or not to purchase new plant and equipment, he is helping to determine the rate of economic progress and is influencing the level of employment and prices. When he decides to

close down a plant or to move it to another location, he may be affecting the economic future. When he decides to build up or reduce inventories, he may be contributing to inflation or accelerating recession. When he changes his wage policy or dividend policy, he may be influencing both the level of employment and the degree of justice achieved in our distribution of income. When he uses the newspaper, radio, and television for advertising or public relations, he may be influencing moral and cultural standards. When he introduces new personnel policies, he may be contributing toward cooperation and understanding between labor and management or he may be reinforcing existing tensions and frictions. When he transacts business in foreign lands, he may be contributing to international tensions or to international understanding.[8]

Because the relationship between firms and the societies in which they operate is symbiotic, because firms are able to combine resources on a scale and with an efficiency that no other human-invented entity can match, and because there is an ethical and moral component to all aspects of business/human decisions, it is vital to understand the role of for-profit firms in society. The behavior of firms (how they do what they do) affects not only our material wellbeing, but all other aspects of our quality of life and, by a large margin, they are the dominant predictor of that outcome − from our experiences at work, to the products we buy, to the air that we breathe; corporations define the lives that we live.

As such, the for-profit firm is cause both for celebration and concern. It is true, for example, that, as a rule, societies that provide more freedom for their for-profit firms to operate will experience more innovation and progress than those societies that do not. It is also true that we should expect this relationship to hold consistently, all else being equal. Of course, however, all else is not equal, which is the reason for writing this book, and today many feel there is more reason than usual for concern:

> Business is the cultural, organizational, and economic superforce in human development. And yet the current state of this social institution is fundamentally flawed: It falls short in its potential to serve our global society. Today's predominant business models drive public companies, for instance, to focus on predictable, short-term shareholder returns that may be detrimental to employees, communities, or the broader social good. They also fail to motivate industries to reduce their environmental impact.[9]

As with many things in life, the relationship between economic freedom and societal progress is not linear. While the correlation is undoubtedly positive, there are limits to the value of untrammeled economic freedom. It does not necessarily hold, for example, that complete freedom for firms equals maximum societal progress. If we did not have controls on the use of toxic chemicals in consumer products, there is plenty of evidence to suggest that some firms would take advantage of consumer ignorance and use those chemicals, irrespective of the consequences for public health. Similarly, there is a reason why we place restrictions on the marketing and sales of products that are deemed to be socially harmful, such as alcohol and tobacco. There are good reasons why we allow firms to emit only certain levels of pollutants into the atmosphere or waste stream; there are also reasons why we pressure firms to curb their marketing to vulnerable segments of society, such as children, and so on, and so on.

Rampant, unrestrained capitalism is unlikely to maximize value, broadly defined. A capitalist system that is constrained through a series of checks and balances, however, promises outcomes that serve a broad set of interests. Firms have micro interests and societies have macro interests. A problem arises, therefore, when the interests of the firm and the interests of society conflict. When this happens, those societies with fewer controls over firms will still experience a large degree of innovation, but it will likely result in a reduction in overall value as firms innovate and bring those innovations to market in ways that suit their short-term interests, but work against the longer-term, competing interests of society. The optimal situation is to have the interests of the firm overlap with the interests of the broader society, with both parties working to generate constructive, mutually beneficial outcomes.

Self-interest and public interest

The mechanism by which the interests of the firm and the interests of society become aligned is through the interactions the firm has with its stakeholders – employees, consumers, suppliers, the government, the media, NGOs, and so on. For example, if I, as a consumer, decide that I want to shop at firms that do not outsource their manufacturing jobs overseas and I actively discriminate in favor of such firms (even if it costs me more to do so), then I am making a statement about the kind of firms that I want in my society. Similarly, if I, as an employee, decide to work for firms that have a diverse workforce and I actively apply for jobs only at such firms (and avoid applying for jobs at less diverse firms), then I am again making a statement about the kind of firms that I want in my society. Now, if I am alone in imposing those values on firms, it will not alter anything. If, however, many other people make the same decisions based on a similar set of values, then such values will quickly become standard operating procedure across the majority of firms. This means that, while there is no longer a differentiation advantage to be gained for firms that implement these practices, there is a significant disadvantage for firms that resist. So, standards evolve and society progresses (or regresses, depending on the nature and extent of the change).

These tradeoffs are resolved via values that are embedded in the decisions the firm and its stakeholders make as they interact. As these values are applied and enforced by stakeholders across the thousands of interactions each firm has with its various constituents on a day-to-day basis, the interests of the firm become more closely aligned with the values of the broader society. As long as the firm is willing to pay attention to the needs and demands of its stakeholders (both internal and external), and those stakeholders are willing to actively shape the society in which they want to live, then it is in the interests of the firm to advance that goal (and its own success) by altering its behavior to match the demands that are placed upon it.

In other words, over time, firms reflect the societies in which they operate (in the same way that politicians reflect the time and context in which they were elected). As organizations, they are not conscious actors so much as mirrors that respond to the values-based constraints placed upon them. If we loosen these constraints, those looser standards will quickly become apparent in the behavior they encourage. Equally, however, if we tighten these constraints, firms will respond quickly and efficiently – simply because it is in their interest to do so. But such an iterative relationship relies on our vigilance if it is to generate the outcomes we say we desire. Less vigilance is consequential, but is something over which we have control.

The logic behind building this argument of empowered actors and fluid checks and balances (which will be developed further over the remaining nine principles), and encouraging executives to adopt it as a managing philosophy, is that it should face less resistance than attempts to coerce for-profit firms to act in ways they perceive to be against their interests. As noted in the Introduction, a core unresolved debate within the CSR community is whether more socially responsible behavior is best encouraged via mandated or incentivized actions. The resolution around which *SVC* is based (taking into account human nature and centuries of economic development) is that firms are more likely to implement CSR genuinely and substantively if they are convinced it is in their self-interest to do so. Central to this argument is the belief that firms are more likely to avoid or try and circumvent legislation if they are compelled to act.

In addition to the idea of voluntary action being more fruitful than coerced action, building an argument around incentivized self-interest is likely to be more successful because the concept of *moral duty* or *ethical values* (over and above those already enshrined in laws and social customs) is extremely difficult to define and standardize. This is true because an ethical standard is less easily enforced – in a free society, there are no *ethics police*. Who gets to decide which morals/values apply and in what situations, for example? And, if I disagree with those morals/values (i.e., if I live by a different set of standards), why should I be forced to comply with them? What will happen if I do not comply with someone else's ethical standards?

Take the debate over whether an employee should be paid a minimum wage or a living wage. While I may think a minimum wage is an ethical compensation (after all, by definition, it has been determined by government to be a sufficient income), you may disagree and, instead, argue that a living wage is ethical, while a minimum wage is unethical.[10] But, since it is legal for me to pay a minimum wage; as long as there are sufficient workers willing to work at that level, my company will continue to operate (and possibly thrive).[11] And, since I am providing employment to workers who are voluntarily choosing to work at that pay level, who is to say that I am being unethical by hiring them? What if, as an employer, I cannot afford to pay wages that are any higher? In that case, would it be more ethical if I hired no one and left those people unemployed? Would it help anyone if I paid higher wages and went out of business? If, however, workers with the skills that I need for a particular job refuse to work for the minimum wage (or consumers refuse to shop there because of the wages that I pay), then the only way my firm will continue to operate is if I raise the wages I am offering. And, importantly in that circumstance, the support from my stakeholders will provide the resources that enable me to do that.

Similarly, is it more *ethical* for me to hire domestic workers in my factory or outsource production to workers overseas? Some would argue that supporting local jobs is ethical, since you are helping reduce unemployment at home, at least in the short term. But, who is to say that is more ethical than hiring a worker overseas, who probably has fewer opportunities and access to fewer resources to improve their life? Well, there is a good chance that, depending on the job and the industry, the overseas worker is underage. But, even if that is true, the ethics of the decision to allow that individual to work depend on the available alternatives. It would be unethical to hire a 16-year-old garment maker, for example, only if a well-resourced school was a realistic alternative. What if, due to financial pressures, the alternative to factory work is prostitution? How does that affect the relative ethics and morality in hiring a local person versus outsourcing work overseas? My point, of course, is only to note that *What is ethical?* and *What is unethical?* are highly complex and relative questions that, once you start to understand the context and different perspectives, do not lead to easily identifiable answers. Where there is consensus, societies should legislate that consensus into legally enforceable standards. Where consensus does not exist, however, your ethics and values differ from mine, and result in measurable variance in behavioral outcomes.

Having said this, it is important to re-emphasize the enlightened approach to management that is central to *SVC*. Managers reading this are taking away the wrong message if they conclude that self-interest is purely reactive – that, as a firm, I will wait for my stakeholders to declare their interests before responding to them and get away with what I can in the meantime. As argued above, a core component of *SVC* is that it is the process that matters – not what a firm does, so much as how it does it. A firm is established to meet specific needs. As in any competitive market, it pays firms to be slightly ahead of the curve in doing so, and the internal culture of the firm and the personal values of the manager help achieve that. To put it crudely, values tell you not to do the stuff you can get away with today but feel uncomfortable about, because there is a good chance you will not be able to get away with it at some future point. Being able to anticipate what stakeholders need tomorrow is therefore as important as understanding what they need today and is central to the firm's ongoing success, even if it means constraining immediate profits. Even better, articulating those needs in a way those stakeholders had not yet envisioned has the potential to generate astounding economic success. As Steve Jobs famously said:

> You can't just ask customers what they want and then try to give that to them. By the time you get it built, they'll want something new.[12]

What is clear from Principle 1 is that enlightened managers working in progressive, for-profit firms are the most effective means to deliver the innovation that drives societal progress.

Summary

Principle 1 states that *Business is social progress*. It argues that the for-profit firm is the most important organizational form because it is best able to convert valuable and scarce resources into products that we demand that, persistently, raise the overall standard of living. The incentive to innovate is central to this process, but innovation occurs elsewhere in society, too. Irrespective of its origin, for-profit firms excel when they seek to bring such innovation to market. Integral to this process are the multitude of decisions, laden with ethical and moral implications, that the firm makes every day. While self-interest is a powerful motivator, value is optimized in its broadest sense when the interests of the firm overlap significantly with the interests of its invested stakeholders. *SVC* represents the mechanism by which these interests are aligned.

Principle 2

Shareholders do not own the firm

> **Key takeaway:** Contrary to popular myth, shareholders are not the legal owners of the firm. Similarly, managers do not have a fiduciary responsibility to maximize shareholder value. Instead, the firm is an independent legal entity that should be run in the interests of its broad set of stakeholders.

As argued in Principle 1, for-profit firms are the most effective way we have devised to advance social wellbeing. Because firms are part of society and society is constructed of multiple components, including firms, the interests of the firm and the interests of society are inextricably interwoven. In other words, business is not a zero-sum exchange, but an ongoing reciprocal relationship between the for-profit firm and its various invested constituents. Together, all of these stakeholders, plus firms, form the broader group that we refer to as *society*. An answer to the fundamental question that we face (*What is the purpose of the for-profit firm in society?*), therefore, is best achieved when the interests of the firm and its stakeholders are aligned.

This iterative relationship stems from the origins of the corporation and the evolution of this organizational form throughout history. In particular, it relates directly to the introduction of *limited liability* in the mid-nineteenth century.[1] Prior to this point, corporate charters were granted by the state as a privilege (rather than a right) and under strict conditions in terms of the projects that were to be completed (e.g., building a bridge or a railroad) and the length of time the corporation was allowed to exist. Importantly, these projects were determined on the basis of perceived societal need, rather than the ability of the firm to make a profit:

> In the legal environment of the 1800s, the state in the initial formulation of corporate law could revoke the charter of a corporation if it failed to act in the public good, and routinely did so. For instance, banks lost their charters in Mississippi, Ohio, and Pennsylvania for "committing serious violations that were likely to leave them in an insolvent or financially unsound condition." In Massachusetts and

New York, charters of turnpike corporations were revoked for "not keeping their roads in repair."[2]

And, when the specified project was completed, the corporation ceased to exist. In short, the corporation existed at the pleasure of the state:[3]

> In 1848, Pennsylvania's General Manufacturing Act set a twenty-year limit on manufacturing corporations. As late as 1903, almost half the states limited the duration of corporate charters to between twenty and fifty years. Throughout the nineteenth century, legislatures revoked charters when the corporation wasn't deemed to be fulfilling its responsibilities.[4]

It is because the fundamental legitimacy of the corporation is grounded in these societal origins (i.e., invented to serve society's needs) that, ultimately, *business* is a social exercise. The introduction of limited liability, however, led directly to a shift in the operating principles of the firm. As profit became the primary purpose, rather than the outcome of a valued and meaningful business, it altered the parameters by which the firm's success is measured. While this shift initially generated many benefits, it has become detrimental over time. Specifically, executives today operate under the assumption that the firm's primary obligation is no longer to the state or society, but instead that it has a legal responsibility to operate in the interests of its owners – its shareholders. While this *belief* that shareholders own the firm is widely shared, there is compelling evidence to suggest it is contrived (a social construction), rather than a legally defined *fact*:[5]

> Conceiving of public shareholders as "owners" may in some instances by a helpful metaphor, but it is never an accurate description of their rights under corporate law. Shareholders possess none of the incidents of ownership of a corporation – neither the right of possession, nor the right of control, nor the right of exclusion – and thus "have no more claim to intrinsic ownership and control of the corporation's assets than do other stakeholders."[6]

Understanding the true nature of the relationship between the firm and its investors is therefore necessary to re-orient firms to act in the interests of society as a whole. In short, it is essential in order to adopt *Sustainable Value Creation (SVC)* as the managing philosophy of a firm.

Limited liability

The great value of limited liability is that it enabled corporations to raise the capital that was needed to finance the infrastructure that fueled the industrial revolution. In particular, limited liability allowed firms to build the railways, canals, and bridges that were central to economic development in the West during the nineteenth century (particularly in the United Kingdom and United States). As such, at least in its original formulation, the idea of shareholders as a firm's owners had some validity because, while stocks were still traded, the primary purpose of shares was to raise capital and provide a return on that investment from the firm to its investors. Over time, however, the shareholder's role and value to the firm has evolved.

Today, on the surface, the relationship between the firm and its shareholders appears unchanged. Many people believe that the primary function of the stock market is for firms to raise the capital they need to finance their business and, indeed, when firms initially list their shares, this transfer of funds from investor to entrepreneur occurs. In reality, however, this initial transaction is only a minor part of the stock market's function. Increasingly, it has evolved into a forum for the subsequent trading of those shares, rather than for their initial offering. This shift represents the difference between a trade for which the firm receives money (the initial listing) to one where it receives no money (a subsequent trade between third parties).

As a firm's shares continue to trade and a track record of performance is established, the share price increasingly becomes a vote of confidence in the firm's current management team and its future potential. In other words, when I buy a share in Apple, I almost certainly buy it not from the company, but from another investor who is seeking to sell that share. The price on which we agree reflects our respective bets on the future success of the company. I buy at a price that I believe is lower than it will be in the future, while the seller sells at a price they believe is higher than it will be in the future. So, we place our respective bets and the trade is made. In the process, however, an important shift has occurred in the primary function of the stock market and of investors who buy and sell shares today, not because they expect to influence a firm's strategic direction but because they hope to profit from the strategic direction that has already been decided by management. Although activist investors occasionally win seats on a board by amassing significant share holdings, these investors are a minority. In reality, most shareholders can only express their opinions about a firm's management by holding, buying, or selling shares.

The consequences of this shift in the underlying relationship between the firm and its shareholders is reflected in the evolving role of stock markets, which are neither efficient (in terms of complete and freely available information guiding capital allocation) nor public (in terms of equal and evenly distributed access). Stock markets have benefits (in terms of liquidity and enabling retirement saving), but it is legitimate to question the overall value they provide. This is especially true today as the majority of trades on any of the major exchanges are made by high-frequency algorithms – computers running programs and holding positions for micro-seconds:

> Each day around 7bn shares worth $320bn change hands on America's stockmarket. Much of that volume is high-frequency trading, in which

stocks are flipped at speed in order to capture fleeting gains. High-frequency traders, acting as middle-men, are involved in half of the daily trading volumes. ... rules-based investors now make the majority of trades. ... The total value of American public equities is $31tn, as measured by the Russell 3000, an index. The three types of computer-managed funds – index funds, ETFs and quant funds – run around 35% of this. Human managers, such as traditional hedge funds and other mutual funds, manage just 24%.[7]

One characteristic of high-frequency trading, therefore, is the sheer volume of activity. While high-frequency trades "comprise half of all trades on the American market [they] submit almost 99% of the orders."[8] Partly this is because the algorithms are able to handle the associated complexity and can arbitrage value in small increments; partly, though, it is because placing a large number of small orders allows high-frequency traders to learn the intentions of other traders in the market and, as a result, trade more advantageously on that information.[9] In addition to volume, another characteristic of high-frequency trading is speed. By positioning themselves between buyer and seller, high-frequency traders can generate massive profits on small margins and extremely large volume. Central to this advantage is being the first to market – the value of which is indicated by the extent to which high-frequency traders are willing to invest in order to gain the slightest of edges over the competition:

> [One] group spent $300m to lay a cable in the straightest possible line from Chicago to New York, cutting through mountains and under car parks, just so the time taken to send a signal back and forth could be cut from 17 milliseconds to 13. In return, the group could charge traders $14m a year to use the line. Traders were willing to shell out those fees because those fractions of a second might generate annual profits of $20 billion.[10]

Almost all of these stock trades are third-party transactions in which the firm receives no capital. The overall effect is to drive a wedge between the interests of the shareholder (return on investment) and the managers of the firm (sustainable competitive advantage). As pools of assets are increasingly managed by a concentrated number of massive investment firms, this wedge grows larger. Take BlackRock, for example, which, along with Vanguard and State Street (the "Big Three"), are now "the largest shareholder in just over 40% of listed American firms,"[11] and are predicted to be "less than a decade away" from managing more than $20 trillion.[12] Firms such as BlackRock (the largest asset manager in the world with "more than $6trn of assets under management")[13] specialize in what are known as *passive* investments, such as exchange-traded funds (ETFs), which attempt to mirror (rather than outperform) the performance of the markets while minimizing fees to their clients.[14] The traders who work for firms like BlackRock therefore have little interest in the day-to-day management of the firms in which they invest. By definition, traders that seek to mirror market performance invest in proportion to the size of each firm in the market, rather than caring necessarily whether Firm A performs better or worse than Firm B.

The combination of high-frequency traders holding positions for microseconds and massive investment funds holding large but passive positions is redefining what it means to be a *shareholder*. In essence, John Maynard Keyes' characterization of financial speculation as "anticipating what average opinion expects the average opinion to be"[15] is truer today than ever before. And, when traders act on behalf of investors, "they're actually in the business of convincing other people that they can anticipate average opinion about average opinion."[16] The cumulative effect is for an individual investor to surrender any claim of *ownership* in favor of managerial control. This trend has been apparent for at least half-a-century:

> under modern conditions of large-scale production great power over the lives of people is centered in the relatively few men who preside over our great corporations. Though the stock ownership of these corporations may be diffused, effective ownership in terms of control resides in management.[17]

In response, some concede that, while shareholders may not control the firm, they still own it. But, does ownership not encompass the ability to control? It is very difficult to think of a definition of *ownership* that does not also include aspects of control or authority over the thing that is owned. The *Oxford English Dictionary*, for example, defines *ownership* as the "act, state, or right of *possessing* something," with *possession* defined as "the state of having, owning, or controlling something."[18] Yet clearly, shareholders do not control the firm.

A legal person

Irrespective of dictionary or intuitive definitions of ownership, what does the law say about the relationship between the firm and its shareholders? Given the extent to which the idea that shareholders are the "legally defined" owners of the firm is believed throughout society, it would follow that such a fact is unambiguously stated in law and demonstrated via legal precedent.[19] In the place of clarity, however, the evidence suggests there is ambiguity:

> This argument [that shareholders own the firm] is based on a misinterpretation of the legal position on the issue of share ownership. ... Once shareholders subscribe to shares in the corporation, payment made in consideration for the shares is considered property of the corporation, and the shareholders are not free to withdraw the sum invested except for payments through dividends, selling their shares, and other permitted means.[20]

Shareholders own shares – a legal contract between the investor and the firm similar to employees, suppliers, and others who also hold legal contracts with the firm. What is becoming increasingly clear is that, while stockholders invest capital in firms (in the same way employees invest time, effort, and skills), they have no greater claim to ownership of those firms than other stakeholders.[21] And, there is a growing number of commentators, such as Martin Wolf in the *Financial Times*, who believe their claim is significantly less than other stakeholders:

> The economic purpose of property ownership is to align rights to control with risk-bearing. The owner of a corner shop should control the business because she is also its chief risk-bearer. Risk, reward and control are aligned. Is it true that the chief risk-bearer in [a publicly-traded corporation] is the shareholder? Obviously not. All those who have stakes in the company that they are unable to hedge bear risks. The most obvious such risk-bearers are employees with firm-specific skills. ... Shareholders, in contrast, can easily hedge their risks by purchasing a diversified portfolio.[22]

Essentially, being a shareholder entitles the owner of that share to a few specific and highly limited rights: they are able to vote (although the practical application of shareholder democracy is weak and narrow); they are able to receive dividends (only as long as the firm is willing to issue them); and they are able to offer their share for sale to a third-party at a time of their choosing. These rights constitute a contractual relationship between the firm and the shareholder, but do not constitute *ownership*. As noted by Eugene Fama, one of the originators of the agency theory of the firm, "Ownership of capital should not be confused with ownership of the firm."[23]

But, if the shareholders do not own the firm, then who does? One of the great advantages of the LLC (Limited Liability Company) form is that the organization is recognized as an independent entity in the eyes of the law (a legal person). As such, the firm, as an artificial person, has many of the rights (although, it seems, fewer of the responsibilities) of a human being or natural person. It can own assets; it can sue and be sued; it can enter into contracts; and, in the U.S., it has the right to freedom of speech (which it exercises by spending money). It is these rights (the right to be sued, in particular) that allow investors to have their legal liability limited to the extent of their investment. In short, the firm is a legal creation that exists, by design, independently of all other actors "and it is the corporation not the individual shareholders, that is liable for its debts."[24]

This concept of the firm as a legal person is established in the subconscious of society in the same way that the idea that firms are owned by their shareholders is also established. The difference between the two is that the idea of the corporation as a person is legally defined, while the idea of shareholders as owners is not. In fact, the unique legal status of corporations is constitutionally protected. Following the Civil War, the Fourteenth Amendment was passed to protect the rights of recently freed African–American slaves. In particular, it stipulates that the states cannot "deprive any person of life, liberty, or property without due process of law." It is via the Fourteenth Amendment that corporations appropriated those rights for themselves.[25] In other words, the U.S. Supreme Court has agreed with the argument that corporations are legally similar to real people and, as such, enjoy similar constitutionally protected rights. The fact that the root of this legal status lies in the Fourteenth Amendment, specifically passed to prevent the ownership of individuals by others, reinforces the idea that the corporation is an independent legal entity.[26]

A similar legal foundation for the idea that shareholders own the firm does not exist, in spite of the popular perception that it is true. In other words, as even supporters of the notion of shareholder primacy note, "shareholder wealth maximization is widely accepted at the level of rhetoric but largely ignored as a matter of policy implementation."[27] The reason for this is that, even if it was an ideal, "the rule of wealth maximization for shareholders is virtually impossible to enforce as a practical matter."[28] As a direct result, under U.S. corporate law, courts are reluctant to intervene in the business decisions of a firm unless there is evidence of fraud, misappropriation of funds, or some other illegal activity. The law is clear that corporations are managed by the board of directors who have "broad latitude to run companies as they see fit."[29] Although shareholders nominally have the right to vote for directors, nominating candidates is extremely difficult and, once elected, directors can ignore shareholder interests. Although shareholders can protest in terms of resolutions at AGMs, "only certain kinds of shareholder votes – such as for mergers or dissolutions – are typically binding. Most are purely advisory":[30]

> The principle that a company's directors should have a free hand to manage its affairs can be traced at least as far back as an 1880 New Hampshire Supreme Court decision. In Charlestown Boot & Shoe Co. vs. Dunsmore, directors won a ruling that shareholders couldn't second guess their decisions, including one to skip insurance on a plant that later burned down. The principle has been adopted by many states, including Delaware, where many large companies are organized.[31]

This *business judgment rule* (see below) is similar to common law in the United Kingdom, which refers to the board and senior managers as the "controlling mind and will" of the company. This finding can be traced back to a 1957 Court of Appeal decision by Lord Denning, in which the judge made a distinction between the hands and brains of a company:

> A company may in many ways be likened to the human body. It has a brain and nerve centre which controls what it does. It also has hands which hold the tools and act in accordance with directions from the centre. Some of the people in the company are mere servants and agents

who are nothing more than hands to do the work. ... Others are directors and managers who represent the directing mind and will of the company and control what it does. The state of mind of those managers is the state of mind of the company.[32]

The legal relationship between the firm and its shareholders is most clearly defined in the event of a bankruptcy – shareholders' claims to the firm's assets lie behind those of bondholders and all other creditors. In theory, shareholders have a claim to the future earned profits of the firm. In reality, that claim is weak, with no right to demand the firm issue dividends or buyback shares if it does not wish to do so. In essence, the reason limited liability is so important (because it enables investors to limit their risk while allowing firms to raise capital from multiple sources) also explains why the shareholder is legally impotent in terms of ownership:[33]

Corporations are universally treated by the legal system as "legal persons" that exist separately and independently of their directors, officers, shareholders, or other human persons with whom the legal entity interacts. ... shareholders do not own corporations; nor do they own the assets of corporations.[34]

Contrary to popular myth, as well as widespread belief among executives and directors,[35] therefore, shareholders do not *own* the corporation.[36] Instead, they *own* a type of security (a legal contract) that is commonly referred to as *stock*. The rights associated with this stock are highly limited; in reality, the value of a share lies largely in its re-sale price, achieved via a transaction on a stock exchange based on third-party perceptions of the firm's future performance potential. As acknowledged, even by shareholder advocates:

Today ... there seems to be substantial agreement among legal scholars and others in the academy that shareholders do not own corporations.[37]

The business judgment rule

This challenge to the idea of shareholders as the legal owners of the firm is gradually becoming established. This process is aided by a compelling argument that there is weak legal precedent, in the U.S. or elsewhere,[38] for the idea that managers and directors have a fiduciary responsibility to place shareholder interests over the interests of other stakeholders:[39]

Contrary to widespread belief, corporate directors generally are not under a legal obligation to maximise profits for their shareholders. This is reflected in the acceptance in nearly all jurisdictions of some version of the business judgment rule, under which disinterested and informed directors have the discretion to act in what they believe to be in the best long term interests of the company as a separate entity, even if this does not entail seeking to maximise short-term shareholder value. Where directors pursue the latter goal, it is usually a product not of legal obligation, but of the pressures imposed on them by financial markets, activist shareholders, the threat of a hostile takeover and/or stock-based compensation schemes.[40]

This core concept within corporate law of deference to directors concerning operational decisions (the *business judgment rule*) is embedded firmly in the U.S., as well as almost all other developed economies, such as the UK:

> courts in the United States have on several occasions clearly stated that directors are not agents of the shareholders but fiduciaries of the corporation. Section 172 of the U.K. Companies Act 2006, moreover, requires directors to act in the way they consider, in good faith, would be most likely to promote the long-term success of the company for the benefits of its members as a whole, heeding the likely consequences of their decisions on stakeholders such as customers, suppliers, and community, not simply shareholders. The Law even allows the board to put the interests of other stakeholders over and above those of shareholders.[41]

The legal foundation for the belief in the primacy of shareholder interests rests largely on a single case decided in 1919 by the Michigan Supreme Court – *Dodge v. Ford Motor Co.*[42] In the case, two brothers, John Francis Dodge and Horace Elgin Dodge (who, together, owned 10% of Ford's shares), sued Henry Ford because of his decision to distribute surplus profit to customers in the form of lower prices for his cars, rather than to shareholders in the form of a dividend. As noted above, however, the value of this case as legal precedent for the idea that the firm must operate in the interests of its shareholders is disputed. As Lynn Stout explains in her analysis of this case, contrary to widespread perceptions and norms, there is no obligation on managers or directors to focus the firm's efforts primarily on maximizing shareholder value:

> *Dodge v. Ford* is … bad law, at least when cited for the proposition that the corporate purpose is, or should be, maximizing shareholder wealth. *Dodge v. Ford* is a mistake, … a doctrinal oddity largely irrelevant to corporate law and corporate practice. What is more, courts and legislatures alike treat it as irrelevant. In the past thirty years, the Delaware courts have cited *Dodge v. Ford* as authority in only one unpublished case, and then not on the subject of corporate purpose, but on another legal question entirely.[43]

More specifically, Stout's empirical analysis of historical case law provides compelling evidence to support her arguments. Not only was the case decided by the Michigan Supreme Court and essentially ignored in Delaware (where the most important points of U.S. corporate law are established), but the legal precedent it represents is more properly understood as a question of the relative responsibilities of majority shareholders (in this case, Ford) toward minority shareholders (in this case, the Dodge brothers).[44] As a result, Stout argues that "we should stop teaching *Dodge v. Ford*"[45] in our universities and business schools as support for a perceived obligation that is neither legally required nor operationally necessary:[46]

> United States corporate law does not, and never has, required directors of public corporations to maximize either share price or shareholder wealth. To the contrary, as long as boards do not use their power to enrich themselves, the law gives them a wide range of discretion to run public corporations with other goals in mind, including growing the firm, creating quality products, protecting employees, and serving the public interest.[47]

There is even precedent to suggest that courts will favor the firm's directors over shareholders when the investors have been deceived, basing investment decisions on the firm's publicly stated goals, even if those statements later turn out to be false.[48] A lack of competence or an honest mistake are not sufficient to override the courts' reluctance to interfere with the running of the firm. Unless it can be proved that the directors acted dishonestly or with the intention to deceive, the business will be allowed to rise or fall on the basis of its operational decisions. Although this issue has been studied and debated by corporate legal scholars, however, it is less well known in the business school. This is important and should change:

> Oddly, no previous management research has looked at what the legal literature says about [shareholder control of the firm], so we conducted a systematic analysis of a century's worth of legal theory and precedent. It turns out that the law provides a surprisingly clear answer: Shareholders do not own the corporation, which is an autonomous legal person. What's more, when directors go against shareholder wishes – even when a loss in value is documented – courts side with directors the vast majority of the time. Shareholders seem to get this. They've tried to unseat directors through lawsuits just 24 times in large corporations over the past 20 years; they've succeeded only eight times. In short, directors are to a great extent autonomous.[49]

Stakeholders, not shareholders

Contrary to popular myth, therefore, shareholders do not own and firm and directors do not have a fiduciary responsibility to act primarily in their interests. As a result, a growing number of legal and corporate governance scholars argue for a return to the driving purpose of a firm being to meet the needs of society, broadly defined. Central to this argument is the idea that firms seek to return value over the medium to long term among all of their stakeholders and avoid the temptation to focus disproportionately on short-term returns to shareholders. The reason why such a narrow focus is counter-productive is that it privileges the interests of a minority (share-holders) over the majority (everyone else)[50] in ways that often do not even benefit the firm.

Pressures from shareholders to maximize results in the short term can be expressed internally within the firm in many ways,[51] "including lower expen-ditures on research and development, an excessive focus on acquisitions rather than organic growth, underinvestment in long-term projects, and the adop-tion of executive remuneration structures that reward short rather than long-term performance."[52] The overall effect is to skew decision-making. Why invest for the medium to long term, for example, when that expenditure will diminish the chances of achieving the more immediate priority – short-term profits? Cutting long-term costs, such as R&D or safety and preventative measures, has the desired effect of increasing profits, which is then reflected in a higher share price.[53] While this immediate accounting profit pleases those investors who have a short-term outlook, such actions constrain the firm's medium to long-term operations.

In order to manage the firm based on a more sustainable business model, one of the most important changes managers must make is to adopt a broader stakeholder perspective. The difference from the CEO's perspective centers on whether the goal is to maximize performance in the short term (the average tenure for a Fortune 500 CEO is about three and a half years) or to preserve the organization for the foreseeable future (10, 15, 20 or more years from now). The focus should be on what Gus Levy, former senior partner of Goldman Sachs, characterized as being "long-term greedy"[54] – the willingness to privilege long-term value over short-term profits. To achieve this, an important step is for firms to adopt policies that better align executive remu-neration with long-term performance drivers that matter to key stake-holders.[55] In addition, firms can de-emphasize short-term results by refusing to issue quarterly earnings reports to investors ("Over three quarters of com-panies still issue such [earnings] guidance").[56] Above and beyond specific policy solutions, however, the key is to deconstruct the idea that there is a legal compulsion to operate the firm in the interests of its shareholders. Once this is achieved, the justification is removed for favoring them over other stakeholders (and, with it, the cause of much of the short-term focus of our economic system):

> As a theoretical matter, the issue of ownership is necessary to a proper understanding of the nature of the corporation and corporate law. As a practical matter, it is an important consideration in the allocation of rights in the corporation: if shareholders are owners, then the balance of rights

will tip more heavily in their favor, and against others, than if they are not. … Because the issue of ownership has the potential to shape all of corporate law and direct the very purpose of corporations, it is of utmost importance.[57]

The value to the firm in understanding this (removing a short-term focus on shareholder interests, and, instead, seeking constructive, trust-based relations with all stakeholders) is that it immediately alters the nature of the decision-making process. If I see interactions with my stakeholders as one-off exchanges (i.e., a short-term perspective), for example, I am likely to prioritize my own interests during negotiations. If I perceive all my interactions as repeat transactions (i.e., I want to build long-lasting relationships), however, then I am more likely to also care about my partners' interests because, if my partners do not value the exchange, it is less likely that they will want to do business with me again in the future.[58]

In other words, the key focus for debate is temporal. Attempts to maximize profits over the short term lead to all the problems that are evident with a narrow focus on shareholder value. If a firm seeks to optimize value over the medium to long term, however, many of those problems dissolve and the process of building meaningful, lasting relations with a broad range of stakeholders becomes central to the mission. It is fundamental to the idea of *SVC* that, by seeking to meet the needs of as broad an array of stakeholders as possible, a firm holds a competitive advantage that can be sustained. Central to achieving this, however, is understanding the true nature of the relationship between the firm and its shareholders and removing the misplaced and inaccurate belief that executives and directors have a legal obligation to make decisions in the interests of shareholders, who are only one of the firm's many stakeholders.[59]

To reiterate, corporate law in the U.S. is clear: No one owns the corporation. It is an independent person in the eyes of the law. This has constitutional grounding in the Fourteenth Amendment, which abolished slavery and granted individuals equal rights (in conjunction with the Thirteenth and Fifteenth Amendments). In short, any claim of shareholder primacy "is flawed in its assumptions, confused as a matter of law, and damaging in practice."[60] This position is supported by the Delaware General Corporation Law,[61] which says the principal of the company is the firm's board of directors, whose fiduciary responsibility is to the organization (and no one else). This is also the basis for limited liability. If you set up a corporation tomorrow and you are the only investor and you are the only employee, you still do not own it. You may have full control, but you do not own it. And, you should not want to own it. The fact that the company is a legal person who can own assets and be sued in court is what prevents you from having full liability. This is an essential and valuable cornerstone of our capitalist system.

Summary

Principle 2 states that *Shareholders do not own the firm*. In reality, nobody owns a firm – it cannot be owned. In addition, executives and directors do not have a fiduciary responsibility to manage the firm primarily in the interests of shareholders. Legally, the corporation is an independent entity (a legal person) with contractual interests. Philosophically, it is the collective effort of the actions and interests of multiple parties, all of whom have a stake in the value creation process. An important step managers can make to reinforce this reality is to resist pressures for short-term performance and, instead, make decisions that are in the medium- to long-term interests of the organization, and all of its stakeholders.

Principle 3

Prioritizing competing stakeholder interests is difficult

> **Key takeaway:** Implementing *SVC* requires the firm to operate in the interests of its stakeholders, broadly defined. While identifying these stakeholders is easy, however, stakeholder theory will only be of practical value when it helps managers prioritize among competing stakeholder interests.

As detailed in Principle 2, shareholders neither own the firm, nor do managers and directors have a legal obligation to run the firm with the primary goal of generating shareholder value. Once managers understand they are free of the mythical obligation to act solely in the interests of the firm's shareholders, they can take a more expansive (and, in terms of the health of the organization, more sustainable) approach to building relations with a much broader range of stakeholders.

This is essential because, although the firm is a legal person, it cannot act alone. A firm is not a sentient actor, but a bundle of contracts (formal and informal) that reflect the aggregated interests of all its stakeholders. If we agree that employees are stakeholders, as well as executives, directors, shareholders, consumers, the government, suppliers, distributors, and so on, then we understand that the firm does not exist independently of these groups. If you take them all away (the executives, directors, and employees, in particular), there is nobody left to act – the firm's substance is derived from the individuals that constitute it. This substance comes from the actions initiated by stakeholders pursuing their specific interests (sometimes competing, sometimes complementary) that intersect within the firm's organizational boundaries via day-to-day operations. This is why stakeholder theory is central to any CSR perspective (really, to any view of the firm), but also explains why it is so important for managers to be able to manage these different interests. To do this, they need to be able to prioritize among stakeholders, on an issue-by-issue basis, in order to create value for most of the firm's stakeholders most of the time.

Stakeholder theory

The success of contemporary stakeholder theory is most often credited to the work of the management and philosophy professor, Ed Freeman. In his important 1984 book, *Strategic Management: A Stakeholder Approach*, he defined a firm's stakeholder as "any group or individual who can affect or is affected by the achievement of the organization's objectives."[1] While Freeman did much to popularize stakeholder theory (particularly in the business school), however, the idea that the "businessman" has responsibilities to a broad range of constituents predates his work by many years. As far back as 1945, for example, Frank Pierce, a director of the Standard Oil Company (New Jersey), argued that a firm's managers have a duty "to act as a balance wheel in relation to three groups of interests – the interests of owners, of employees, and of the public, all of whom have a stake in the output of industry."[2] In 1951, Frank Abrams, the CEO of Standard Oil, extended this argument:

> Business firms are man-made instruments of society. They can be made to achieve their greatest social usefulness … when management succeeds in finding a harmonious balance among the claims of the various interested groups: the stockholders, employees, customers, and the public at large.[3]

Similarly, in 1953, Howard Bowen discussed the idea of the "participation of workers, consumers, and possibly of other groups in business decisions."[4] And more specifically, in 1964, Eric Rhenman defined the *stakeholders* in an organization as "the individuals and groups who are depending on the firm in order to achieve their personal goals and on whom the firm is depending for its existence."[5] As is therefore apparent, the idea of the *stakeholder* has been around for a while. While Freeman did not claim to have invented the concept,[6] his contribution was pivotal for two main reasons: first, he rendered the concept relatable in meaning and action for business practitioners; and second, he promoted the concept within the academic community in general, and the field of management in particular. As a result, a stakeholder is widely understood to be a group or individual with a self-defined interest in the activities of the firm.[7] A core component of the intellectual argument driving *Sustainable Value Creation* (*SVC*) is that it is in a firm's best interests to meet the needs and expectations of as many of these stakeholders as often as possible.

A stakeholder

An individual or organization that is affected by the firm (either voluntarily or involuntarily), and possesses the capacity and intent to affect the firm.

In identifying and understanding the interests of its core stakeholders, the firm may find it helpful to divide these constituents into three separate groups: *organizational* stakeholders (internal to the firm), and *economic* and *societal* stakeholders (external to the firm). Together, these three kinds of stakeholders form a metaphorical concentric set of circles with the firm and its organizational stakeholders at the center within a larger circle that signifies the firm's economic stakeholders. Both of these circles sit within the largest outside circle, which represents the firm's operating context and its societal stakeholders.

Within this overall classification, all possible actors fit primarily into one of the three stakeholder groups. First, stakeholders exist within the organization and include the firm's employees, managers, and directors. Taken together, these internal stakeholders constitute the operational core of the organization and, therefore, should be its primary concern. Second are economic stakeholders that include the firm's shareholders, consumers, creditors, and competitors. The interactions these stakeholders have with the firm are driven primarily by financial concerns. As such, these stakeholders fulfill an important role as the interface between the organization and its larger social context in ways that create bonds of accountability. Third are those stakeholders that constitute the broader political and social environment in which the firm operates. Examples of these stakeholders include government agencies and regulators, the media, and the broader communities in which the firm operates (including non-governmental organizations, NGOs, and other activist groups). These societal stakeholders are essential for the firm in terms of providing the legitimacy necessary for it to survive over the medium to long term.[8]

This model of concentric circles indicates the primary association of each actor, but it is important to recognize that almost all stakeholders exist simultaneously as multiple stakeholder types with network ties among each of them, as well as with the firm.[9] A company's employees, for example, are primarily organizational stakeholders, but are also occasional customers of the firm, as well as being members of the society in which the firm operates. The government that regulates the firm's industry, however, is only a societal stakeholder and has no direct economic relationship with the company (beyond the taxes it levies and the subsidies it pays), nor is it a formal part of the organization. The firm's economic stakeholders represent the interface between the organizational and societal stakeholders. A firm's customers are, first and foremost, economic stakeholders. They are not organizational stakeholders (unless they are also employees), but they are part of the society in which the firm operates. They are also one of the primary means by which the firm delivers its product and interacts with its society. Without the economic interface, a firm loses its mechanism of accountability, and therefore its legitimacy, over the long term.

The three layers of a firm's stakeholders all sit within the larger context of a business environment that is shaped by macro-level forces such as globalization, climate change, and the increasing affluence that is driving development and raising the expectations different societies place on their for-profit firms, worldwide.

Prioritizing stakeholders

In spite of its importance to the concept of *SVC*, stakeholder theory can only be of value to the firm when it accounts fully for the dynamic environment in which business is conducted. In particular, while stakeholder theory is conceptually useful for managers in terms of defining those groups with an interest in the firm's operations, it has been much less instructive in providing a practical roadmap for implementation. There is a reason for this – while accounting for a broader range of interests is valuable, it also complicates a firm's decisions more often than not:

> A single goal, such as maximum profit, is simple and reasonably concrete. But when several goals are introduced and businessmen must sometimes choose from among them (e.g., greater immediate profit vs. greater company security, or good labor relations vs. low-cost production, or higher dividends vs. higher wages), then confusion and divided counsel are sometimes inevitable.[10]

In short, while identifying stakeholders is easy, prioritizing among stakeholder interests is extremely difficult, and stakeholder theory has been largely silent on this essential issue. Partly this is because the process is so idiosyncratic (firms have different stakeholders who see each action as more or less important), but mostly it is because the interests are so compelling and conflict so often. What is required is a framework that can guide managers on how and when to prioritize stakeholder interests. As a first step in this process, managers need to define the firm's operating context in terms of issues that evolve and stakeholders that compete. Accounting for this dynamic reality, relative to the strategic interests of the firm, will help managers decide how to prioritize among stakeholders. This is essential because stakeholders have claims on activities that range across the firm's operations. Yet, stakeholder theory will remain merely an interesting intellectual exercise until it can help tease apart what John Mackey (the founder of Whole Foods Market) describes as the complex demands stakeholders continuously place on his company:

> Customers want lower prices and higher quality; employees want higher wages and better benefits and better working conditions; suppliers want to give fewer discounts and want you to pick up more of their products; communities want more donations; governments want higher taxes; investors want higher dividends and higher stock prices – every one of the stakeholders wants more, they always want more.[11]

Each stakeholder group "will define the purpose of the business in terms of its own needs and desires, and each perspective is valid and legitimate."[12] As such, it is essential for the firm to be able to identify any potential conflict and, where possible, act to mitigate the potential operational threat. In other words, the businesses most likely to succeed in today's rapidly evolving global marketplace will be those best able to adapt to their dynamic environment by balancing the conflicting interests of multiple stakeholders. It can even be argued that, at its core, the fundamental "job of management is to maintain an equitable and working balance among the claims of the various ... interest groups" that are directly affected by the firm's operations.[13] Just because an individual or organization merits inclusion in a firm's list of relevant stakeholders, however, does not compel the firm (either legally or logically) to comply with every demand that they make. Doing so would be counterproductive as the business would be forced to spend all its time addressing these different demands and negotiating among stakeholders with diametrically opposed requests. A key function of the ability to prioritize stakeholder interests, therefore, is determining which stakeholders warrant the firm's attention and when.

The concentric circles of organizational, economic, and societal stakeholders discussed above provide an initial guide to prioritization. By identifying the firm's key stakeholders *within* each category, managers can prioritize the needs and interests of certain groups over others. In addition, *among* categories, as a general rule, stakeholders decrease in importance to the firm the further they are removed from core operations. Implicit in this discussion, therefore, is the idea that organizational stakeholders are a firm's most important set of constituents. Organizational stakeholders are followed in importance by a firm's economic stakeholders, who provide it with the economic capital to survive. Finally, a firm's societal stakeholders deliver it with the social capital that is central to the firm's legitimacy and long-term validity, but are of less immediate importance in terms of day-to-day operations.

In seeking to prioritize its stakeholders, however, a firm needs to keep two key points in mind: First, no organization can afford to ignore consistently the interests of an important stakeholder, even if that group is less important in the relative hierarchy of stakeholders or is removed from day-to-day operations. A good example of this is the government, which is a societal stakeholder and, therefore, is in theory less important than an organizational or economic stakeholder. It would not be wise, however, for a firm to ignore the government repeatedly in relation to an important issue that enjoys broad societal support. Given that the government has the power to constrain or support industries in ways that affect profit levels dramatically, it is only rational that firms should be constantly aware of the government's basic needs and requests.

Second, it is vital to remember that the relative importance of stakeholders will differ from firm-to-firm, from issue-to-issue, and from time-to-time. And, depending on these factors, the change in relative ordering can be dramatic. As such, addressing the fluctuating needs of stakeholders and meeting them wherever possible is essential for firms to survive in today's dynamic business environment. In order to do this, it is important that managers have a framework that will enable them to prioritize stakeholder interests for a given issue and account for those expectations in formulating a strategic response.

The key to building such a framework revolves around three moving parts: the *firm*, the *issue*, and the *stakeholder*. First, the *firm*. Any for-profit organization has strategic interests that determine the industries in which it operates and the products or services that it produces. In addition, the firm has market goals that outline future levels of performance that it deems both attainable and desirable (such as percentage market share or a particular level of sales). Together, these strategic interests and market goals determine the firm's operational priorities. With this benchmark in mind, managers are able to gauge the strategic relevance of any particular issue.

Second, the *issue*. The key factor with any issue that arises is the extent to which it is relevant to the firm's operational priorities. There has been some useful work in this area by Simon Zadek (founder and CEO of the consultancy AccountAbility) that firms can use to evaluate which issues pose the greatest potential opportunity and danger.[14] First, Zadek identifies the five stages of learning that organizations go through "when it comes to developing a sense of corporate responsibility."[15] Then, he combines these five stages of learning with four stages of intensity "to measure the maturity of societal issues and the public's expectations around the issues."[16] The maximum danger, Zadek argues, is for companies that are in defensive mode when facing an institutionalized issue, as they will be ignoring something that potentially poses a significant threat to their business. A firm that continues to deny the existence of climate change, for example, falls into this category. In contrast, those businesses that are promoting industry-wide adoption of standard practices in relation to a newly emerging issue stand to gain the maximum economic and social value for their effort (notwithstanding the risks involved). Even more effective, for those firms willing to take a bold stand on "issues that are contested enough to feel hot, but that have pretty strong consensus from the tastemakers, mavens and social-media influencers of the day," they both help move the idea to the mainstream, while positioning themselves to reap the benefits when it arrives.[17] Once the firm has established an issue as operationally relevant and worked out what position it favors, the next step is to identify those stakeholders that are most affected.

Third, the *stakeholder*. In addition to identifying the importance of a particular issue, the firm must account for its various stakeholders. A firm's stakeholder relations will vary within stakeholders and across issues; they will also vary within issues and across stakeholders. In other words, each stakeholder will have a number of issues that it values. The range of issues will not be valued equally, however, with some prioritized as more important than others. Similarly, for each issue the firm faces, its different stakeholders will have different positions, pushing the firm to respond in one way or another (or another). The firm's ability to understand how important an issue is to any one stakeholder, and how its stakeholders will vary in response to any one issue, will depend on the depth of the relationship already established. It is a key aspect of stakeholder theory in implementation that any firm is better placed to understand its stakeholders if it has already established strong relationships based on trust. If the firm is contacting a stakeholder for the first time only in response to a crisis, its outreach is likely to be less well received. If, however, the firm has an established relationship and is already aware of the needs and positions of the stakeholder, when a crisis arrives, the potential for a value-added solution is higher.

A decision-making model

Once the three factors (firm, issue, and stakeholder) have been considered independently, it is necessary for the manager to combine them on an ongoing basis to determine the appropriate response. This is achieved by considering the three factors in terms of four dimensions: *Strategic relevance, Issue evolution, Stakeholder motivation,* and *Operational impact*. *Strategic relevance* captures how important an issue is to the firm – in other words, how proximal it is to the firm's core competency or source of competitive advantage. *Issue evolution* captures the extent to which the issue has become institutionalized – in other words, the extent to which it has become accepted business practice. *Stakeholder motivation* captures how important the issue is to each stakeholder – in other words, how likely that group is to act in response. And, *Operational impact* captures the extent to which a particular stakeholder group can affect firm operations – in other words, the stakeholder's ability to damage reputation, diminish earnings, or demotivate employees.

The extent to which a firm should act in response to a stakeholder concern about a particular issue, therefore, is determined by the interaction of these four dimensions.[18] The goal is to build a multistep process by which managers can account for variance in the strategic interests of the firm, the evolution of each issue, the motivation of the stakeholder(s), and the potential operational impact of any response. The resulting analysis enables managers to decide how best to prioritize stakeholder concerns and when to act. Importantly, this framework should be embedded within a culture of outreach to stakeholders that allows firms to understand their evolving concerns and assess which issues are more or less important to which group. It also should be repeated on a regular basis since any issue will continue to evolve and stakeholders' interests will adapt, accordingly. Ultimately, when the firm's strategic interests are relevant, an issue is important, stakeholders are motivated, and there is the potential for damage due to intransigence, the firm is compelled to act and act quickly to protect its interests and preserve its relations with stakeholders. This iterative process can be summarized in a seven-step model of stakeholder prioritization that empowers managers to analyze the firm's operating environment on an ongoing basis:

1   **Identify** and engage the set of stakeholders relevant to the firm.
2   **Scan** the environment to identify relevant issues as they arise and evolve.
3   **Analyze** any controversial issue through the filter of the firm's strategic interests.
4   **Prioritize** among competing stakeholder interests in relation to the issue at hand.
5   **Act** while seeking to satisfy as many stakeholders as possible, in order of priority.
6   **Evaluate** the effect of the action to optimize the outcomes for the firm and its stakeholders.
7   **Repeat** regularly and when necessary.

Following these seven steps maximizes the value of a stakeholder perspective for the firm. The process can be applied to identify stakeholder concerns on either an issue-by-issue basis (i.e., a single issue and multiple stakeholders) or a stakeholder-by-stakeholder basis (i.e., a single stakeholder and multiple issues), depending on the firm's strategic interests. Importantly, this model is also both proactive and reactive. It constitutes a tool that managers can use either to anticipate or respond to stakeholder concerns in relation to both opportunities (adding value) and threats (avoiding harm). Ultimately, the goal is to ensure the firm's interests are protected, while also creating value by meeting the needs of most of its stakeholders most of the time (and all of its stakeholders at least some of the time).

Summary

Principle 3 states that, while identifying stakeholders is easy, *Prioritizing competing stakeholder interests is difficult*. It lays out the broad ideas behind stakeholder theory, which is the intellectual backbone of *SVC*. Importantly, however, it also extends stakeholder theory by moving beyond merely defining a firm's stakeholders to developing a seven-step process of prioritization as a decision-making tool managers can use to extract the maximum value of a stakeholder perspective. It is the intersection of the firm's strategic interests, the evolution of a particular issue, and the stakeholder's motivations to respond (and the impact those responses can have) that determine the need for the firm to act.

Principle 4

CSR is a stakeholder responsibility

> **Key takeaway:** CSR will only work if firms are rewarded for acting and punished for failing to act. As such, while CSR includes a *responsibility* for a firm to meet the needs and demands of its stakeholders, the stakeholders themselves have an equal, if not more important, *responsibility* to hold the firm to account.

As illustrated by Principle 3, business is a collective enterprise that is defined by the firm's stakeholder relationships. A firm that is acting responsibly is seeking to create value for all of these stakeholders. In doing so, that firm is also acting in its own best interests, as measured over the medium to long term. But, within this complex web of complementary and conflicting relations, exactly whose responsibility is CSR? The term *Corporate Social Responsibility* misleadingly suggests that the burden rests solely (or even largely) with the firm.

Corporate social responsibility

The entirety of CSR can be discerned from the three words this phrase contains: *corporate*, *social*, and *responsibility*. CSR covers the relationship between corporations (or other for-profit firms) and the societies with which they interact. CSR defines society in its broadest sense and, on many levels, to include all stakeholders that maintain an ongoing interest in the organization's operations. And, as interpreted by the majority of advocates, CSR also includes the responsibilities that the firm has to these varied constituent groups. What this discussion ignores, however, is an understanding of where the motivation for socially responsible behavior comes from. Should corporations act responsibly because they are convinced of the moral argument for doing so (irrespective of the financial implications of their actions), or should they act responsibly because it is in their self-interest? What is the point of a firm acting responsibly if its key stakeholders do not care sufficiently to pay the costs that are often associated with such actions?[1] Unless business suffers as a result of the refusal to act, should firms be expected to change?

Two points are worth emphasizing here: First, for-profit firms are efficient organizations, but managers have no special powers to foresee the future. In spite of this, much of the CSR debate has focused on demanding that firms act proactively out of a social, moral, or ethical duty. In other words, managers are being asked to take a leap of faith – that, if they act *responsibly* (whatever that means), business success will follow. The label *CSR* itself talks about the social responsibility of *corporations* without understanding that, often, there are no meaningful consequences for firms that do not act *responsibly* and that, in contrast, they are often rewarded economically for not doing so. Because of this, firms are reluctant to risk their future viability implementing a business model (and the accompanying set of products and services) that does not have an established market demand. While every manager seeks to be ahead of the curve, in reality, there is as much danger in being too far ahead of the curve as there is in being behind it.[2] It is important for us to remind ourselves that for-profit firms are mirrors to society and, as such, they *react* to stakeholder concerns/needs far more effectively than they *anticipate* those concerns and needs.

Second, having a *responsibility* to do something means there is a consequence to not doing it. No consequence, no responsibility. In order for a responsibility to be enforced, therefore, someone or something must hold the firm to account.[3] If this does not happen, then compliance will vary according to the individual actor's set of personal beliefs and values. In other words, for CSR to work effectively, stakeholders need to act – they need to shape the behavior they want to see from firms in terms of what they feel is important. They then must enforce these standards and encourage the behavior they seek by backing up their demands with meaningful commitment and actively discriminating in the relations they build. For consumers, for example, this requires them to educate themselves about their purchase decisions and be willing to pay higher prices where the consequences of their demands raise costs (and therefore prices). This same approach and equal responsibility apply to all of the firm's stakeholders, such as employees (seek firms with progressive policies and diverse workplaces), government (enforce laws and regulations), suppliers (build constructive, productive ties), the media (investigative journalism focusing on abuses of power), and so on. By acting in this way, stakeholders convey to the firm the message that it is in the organization's self-interest to act in a particular way, whether it would have done so voluntarily (i.e., in the absence of such pressures), or not.

In short, existing discussions around CSR have focused almost exclusively on the responsibilities of business, while ignoring the responsibilities of the firm's stakeholders to demand the kind of behavior they deem to be *socially responsible*. In essence, we get the firms we deserve, just like we get the politicians we deserve. If there is a *problem*, it is with us, rather than the firms we create. If the firm's stakeholders are unwilling to set standards for firms and then enforce them, firms instead will respond with whatever behavior finds success in the market.[4]

Corporate stakeholder responsibility

The philosophy underpinning *Sustainable Value Creation* (*SVC*) is clear that CSR is not only a corporate responsibility. Stakeholders share an interest in optimizing societal outcomes that add value, broadly defined. As a result, they carry an equal, if not more important, responsibility to hold firms to account for their actions. The concept of corporate *stakeholder* responsibility is therefore an essential addition to any definition of CSR that fits within the *SVC* framework.[5]

A new definition of CSR

A view of the *corporation* and its role in *society* that assumes a *responsibility* among firms to meet the needs of their stakeholders and an equal (if not more important) *responsibility* among stakeholders to hold firms to account for their actions.

The change in emphasis that forms the core of this definition is subtle, but the implication for our understanding of what CSR means is radical. To this end, it is worth keeping two points in mind: First, this reciprocal relationship does not remove the moral and ethical dimensions of economic exchange. On the contrary, these factors are embedded in the decisions all stakeholders take in determining which firms to engage with and which actions to endorse. As such, this reconceptualization of CSR shifts the role of morals and ethics in the debate away from absolute standards that are imposed artificially on firms, toward the relative values of each stakeholder that, together, constitute the convoluted environment to which firms have to operate, every day.

Second, this division of responsibilities should not be seen as a burden, but as empowering stakeholders to create the society in which they want to live. Contrary to how they are often presented, firms are neither inherently evil nor divinely angelic. As discussed in Principle 3, firms should not be anthropomorphized – they cannot be separated from the aggregated interests of their collective set of stakeholders. Brands and companies are inert – it is the people inside them that bring them to life. The for-profit firm is a group of individuals that, collectively, reflects the values of those individuals. In the same way that we get the politicians we deserve (by electing them), the way we (as stakeholders) manage our relations with firms generates directly the companies that dominate our economies. As such, the firm's stakeholders need to uphold the values and behavior that they say they want firms to implement:

> One report showed that ensuring good working conditions would add less than one dollar to the price of a pair of blue jeans. But despite

responding to surveys that they care about ethics, shoppers refuse to pay more. In one study, only half of customers chose a pair of socks marked "Good Working Conditions" even when they were the same price as an unmarked pair; only one quarter of customers paid for the socks when they cost 50 percent more.[6]

In short, if we want to change firm behavior, it is incumbent on us (all stakeholders, not only consumers) to take responsibility for the consequences of our actions and decisions. Firms are largely reactive and will respond, efficiently, to the signals we send. In a system of checks and balances (both formal and informal), it is incumbent on all parties to play their respective roles. To date, firms have been reluctant to change and stakeholders have been reluctant to enforce the leverage they possess. Until firms become more responsive and stakeholders become more proactive, substantive change will be slow in coming.

Stakeholder democracy

As these boundaries of acceptable behavior are formed, it is the responsibility of firms to adhere to them, but it is also the responsibility of the firms' stakeholders to enforce them. The outcome of this iterative process is akin to a form of stakeholder democracy:

> The duty of business in a democracy is not merely to meet its social responsibilities as these are defined by businessmen, but rather to follow the social obligations which are defined by the whole community through the give-and-take of public discussion and compromise.[7]

In reality, the way that we differentiate between private sector motivations and public sector demands is usually via the pursuit of profit. But, does that really distinguish different types of behavior? Another way of expressing the balancing act between conflicting stakeholder interests is the push and pull of market forces. While markets are normally thought of in terms of exchanges quantified in monetary value, this concept can be expanded to include a firm's relationships with all of its stakeholders, but valued in different ways. Each stakeholder brings different resources to the exchange in ways that can be expressed as opportunities or threats to the firm. As the firm responds to these forces, different outcomes are shaped that, ultimately, match the desires of all parties involved. A good example of a company that actively institutionalizes this mutually dependent relationship is Patagonia, whose Product Lifecycle Initiative represents:

> a unique effort to include consumers in Patagonia's vision of environmental responsibility. An internal document articulated that reducing Patagonia's environmental footprint required a pledge from both the

company and its customers. The initiative thus consisted of a mutual contract between the company and its customers to "reduce, repair, reuse, and recycle" the apparel that they consumed.[8]

As mentioned in Principle 2, the history of the modern-day company is embedded in its foundation as a tool to serve society's purposes. Although the emphasis in the company-society relationship has shifted over time, the idea that the corporation is a tool that serves society's interests remains fundamentally intact. In short, if capitalism is no longer serving our interests well, it is because we are not using it correctly. More specifically, we are sending firms the wrong signals; and those signals relate directly to our collective set of values.

The idea that firms are imposing $5 T-shirts on us, for example, greatly misrepresents the way markets operate. If we tell firms with our purchase decisions (and materialistic values) that with our $30 we want to buy six T-shirts at $5 each rather than two T-shirts at $15 each, then that is what the market will provide. This is not merely an economic decision, however, but one that is laden with values that have monumental consequences for the kind of society in which we live – one that values quantity over quality, material goods over holistic wellbeing, and short-term comfort over long-term sustainability. If, in contrast, we were willing to buy two T-shirts at $15 each, that would have consequences that would revolutionize our economy (fewer workers in the apparel industry, but better conditions and higher quality T-shirts, for example). Just because we can make T-shirts for $5 each does not mean that we have to – it is a reality that we create. It is essential to the ideas underpinning *SVC* that we understand that our consumption decisions (as in all stakeholder relations with the firm) represent our values in action. Firms are not actively choosing to supply $5 T-shirts so much as they are responding to our demand for such products.[9] If we want the market to change, therefore, we are likely to be more successful if we change the collective set of values that the market reflects (i.e., change ourselves), rather than trying to change the centuries-old economic principles on which the market and for-profit firms operate.

In other words, the argument constructed in this book is not an absolution of the ethical responsibilities of the business executive, but instead a call for those responsibilities to be enforced by the firm's stakeholders (including its managers) who, collectively, have the power to shape the organizational behavior they wish to see. The result of a system that is characterized by tension among competing interests, with give and take on both sides, is a more democratic distribution of the overall value embedded within that system. As Howard Bowen noted back in 1953:

> In a rapidly growing society, even if industry is predominantly competitive, there is nothing to prevent the society from receiving part of its increasing product in the form of better working conditions, shorter

hours, greater security, greater freedom, better products, etc. Gains need not be realized solely in the form of a greater flow of final goods and services. The rising standard of living may consist not alone in an increasing physical quantity of goods and services, but also in improved conditions under which these goods and services are produced.[10]

Increasingly, the tools are becoming available that enable stakeholders to embrace this proactive role. Another way of saying this is that we no longer have an excuse for failing to act. The internet provides access to the information we need to make values-based judgments on the policies and operating procedures of the firms with which we interact. Moreover, the price of communication has been lowered essentially to zero, which enables us to mobilize in ways that counteract the power previously held only by governments or corporations. The overall effect of the encroachment of the internet into every aspect of our lives is to cause firms to lose control over the flow of information. The rise of social media has broken down barriers in ways that alter how stakeholders interact with firms. While firms can benefit from increased communication and data (to increase efficiencies and market-test products, for example), this technology also hands stakeholders a tool they can use to take direct action and hold firms to account. When we demand more and demonstrate a willingness to sacrifice in order to obtain it, the firm is the most rapid and efficient mechanism to meet that demand. There is plenty of evidence to suggest that stakeholder activism is effective. *SVC* calls for an expanded sense of responsibility among all stakeholders to ensure such activism becomes the norm, rather than the exception.

The ideal ecosystem in which business and society co-exist consists of a constant back-and-forth between the self-interest of the business minority and the collective interest of the majority. As society's interests evolve, the resulting external pressures on firms increasingly reflect this change. As these pressures rise, it becomes apparent to the manager that their self-interest lies in conforming to these external expectations. Similarly, as businesses innovate and introduce new products and services to society that shape how we interact with each other, so these changes challenge existing norms and expectations in ways that inform how we live our lives. Understanding that all parties in our economic system help identify this point of balance is essential to creating an economic system that optimizes total value.

As a mirror to the collective set of values that make up society, firms react to the signals its stakeholders send. It is when those signals become mixed or we fail to enforce the behavior we have previously said we want that problems can emerge. The temptation to substitute short-term profits for necessary safety steps, for example, led to a change in culture at BP and a series of serious accidents, from Alaska, to Texas, to the Gulf of Mexico. If the firm's stakeholders had enforced their oversight (e.g., government inspections, partner operating procedures, employee whistleblowing, etc.), these hugely consequential accidents would have been prevented. Even viable companies that produce legal products (such as the tobacco and gun industries often vilified by CSR advocates) exist only due to stakeholder support. If we feel these companies do more harm than good, then it is the responsibility of government to make their products illegal or customers and employees to boycott them. Stakeholders have it in their collective power to shape the firms we want to populate our economies. Firms are not to blame for profiting by selling products that their collective set of stakeholders say that they value.

Within this framework, an ethics or CSR transgression committed by a firm represents a failure of stakeholder oversight – a breakdown in collective vigilance. Whether as a result of lapsed government or media oversight, executive fraud, consumer ignorance, employee silence, or supplier deceit, a *transgression* (which, by definition, is only a socially constructed assessment of right and wrong) occurs when the firm's stakeholders fail to hold it to account. In other words, the firm violates our collective determination of what constitutes *responsible* behavior.

Rather than favoring a form of unregulated capitalism, therefore, which has been roundly (and correctly) criticized for causing economic mayhem in recent decades, the core argument in this book calls for an expanded form of regulation – stakeholder engagement. Rather than rely on legislatures merely to constrain business via restrictive laws (a necessary but insufficient stakeholder action), however, an effective and comprehensive form of corporate *stakeholder* responsibility, in which all stakeholders act to hold firms to account, will generate a market-based system of checks and balances formed around individual values. As such, this web of complex interests acts as a curb on unlimited power; it also provides unbounded opportunity for the firm that is sufficiently progressive to meet and exceed the expectations of its stakeholders. The ultimate effect will be to ensure capitalism is tailored more toward broader, societal interests, rather than narrow, individual or corporate interests.

In this sense, *SVC* is not a passive doctrine; it is highly empowering and potentially revolutionary. True, it is working within the current system, utilizing a firm's pursuit of profit and individuals' self-interest to achieve its goals; but the subtle shifts that it advocates seek to generate very different outcomes throughout society.

Summary

Principle 4 states that *CSR is a stakeholder responsibility*. If we are to achieve the socially responsible outcomes we say we seek, it is essential that all parties (the business and each of its stakeholder groups) play their part. While firms have a responsibility (founded in self-interest) to accommodate, wherever possible, the needs and concerns of their stakeholders, each stakeholder group has a responsibility (founded in self-preservation and social progress) to shape firms' behavior through the expectations that it conveys via meaningful engagement. This *stakeholder* responsibility is equally as important (if not more so) as the responsibility of the firm.

Principle 5

Market-based solutions are optimal

Key takeaway: In general, market forces generate superior outcomes to alternative means of allocating scarce and valuable resources, such as government mandate. While stakeholders have an interest in shaping the behavior of firms, the mechanism by which this occurs most effectively is the market.

As reflected in Principle 4, business is a collaborative exercise. It is in society's best interests to encourage capitalism because for-profit firms are able to foster social progress above and beyond any other organizational form in any other economic system. It is also in society's interests, however, to shape the economic behavior of firms by holding them to account for their actions – a *stakeholder democracy* that ensures it is in firms' best interests to seek to accommodate the needs and interests of all stakeholders. This system of checks and balances works best within a capitalist economic system, where enterprise drives innovation, which promotes progress:

> it's multinational corporations, and not governments or non-profits, that have the vast human and financial capital, advanced technology, international footprint, market power and financial motivation to solve the world's most daunting problems.[1]

Imperfect markets

The core idea around which Principle 5 is built is that markets trump all other known means by which scarce and valuable resources are allocated on a society-wide basis.[2] The beauty of the market, in large part, is its chaotic complexity, where structure somehow emerges out of a multitude of micro-level individual decisions that aggregate into a stable macro-economic system. As Friedrich Hayek noted long ago:

> We are led – for example by the pricing system in market exchange – to do things by circumstances of which we are largely unaware and which

produce results that we do not intend. In our economic activities we do not know the needs which we satisfy nor the sources of the things which we get. Almost all of us serve people whom we do not know, and even of whose existence we are ignorant; and we in turn constantly live on the services of other people of whom we know nothing. All this is possible because we stand in a great framework of institutions and traditions – economic, legal, and moral – into which we fit ourselves by obeying certain rules of conduct that we never made, and which we have never understood in the sense in which we understand how the things that we manufacture function.[3]

Market freedoms are particularly efficient in contrast to government mandate. In part, this is due to the lack of expertise and local knowledge that a central body, by definition, does not have: "Soviet bureaucrats sitting in Moscow, for example, could not possibly know enough to dictate to farmers in individual fields about how to plant their crops."[4] But, it also reflects the powerful ability of the market (via the pursuit of profit) to mobilize resources and incentivize human creativity in ways that alternative motivations, such as altruism and public service, cannot match:

> Johnson Controls joined real-estate firm Jones Lang LaSalle to retrofit the Empire State Building for energy efficiency in 2012. The Clinton Climate Initiative and Rocky Mountain Institute also collaborated on the project. The groups estimate the project will cut energy costs by 38%, saving $4.4m annually and reducing carbon emissions by 105,000 metric tons over 15 years. Given that the building sector consumes up to 40% of the world's energy, energy efficiency is key to reducing our energy use. Retrofitting for energy efficiency is good for the world, while also generating profit for Johnson Controls. The power of financial motivation … solved this problem.[5]

In contrast, the cumulative effects of excessive micro management by governments, as Milton Friedman dryly noted, can be widespread inefficiency and distorted incentives: "If you put the federal government in charge of the Sahara Desert, in 5 years there'd be a shortage of sand." While an exaggeration, to be sure, it is also instructive as a cautionary tale. The history of humankind provides substantial evidence that, while the government has a vital role to play in delivering certain services (such as national defense) and creating the boundaries within which economic exchange can thrive (such as a stable legal system), it is via the spirit of free enterprise that innovation flourishes and poverty is diminished. In Milton Friedman's words again:

> The great achievements of civilization have not come from government bureaus. Einstein didn't construct his theory under order from a bureaucrat. Henry Ford didn't revolutionize the automobile industry that way.

In the only cases in which the masses have escaped from [grinding poverty], the only cases in recorded history, is where they have had capitalism and largely free trade. If you want to know where the masses are worst off, it is exactly in the kinds the societies that depart from that. So the record of history is absolutely crystal clear, that there is no alternative way so far discovered of improving the lot of the ordinary people that can hold a candle to the productive activities that are unleashed by a free enterprise system.[6]

In spite of the demonstrated power of markets to build wealth and promote social progress, it is also true that, in application, markets are inherently flawed. Markets, for example, have the ability to misallocate resources (the reason why CEOs are overpaid), skew priorities (the reason why externalities exist), and focus on the short term (the reason why stock prices fluctuate sporadically). As another Nobel Prize-winning economist, Joseph Stiglitz, notes:

Perfect competition should drive profits to zero, at least theoretically, but we have monopolies and oligopolies making persistently high profits. C.E.O.s enjoy incomes that are on average 295 times that of the typical worker, a much higher ratio that in the past, without any evidence of a proportionate increase in productivity.[7]

These flaws arise due to the fact that markets (like governments) are enacted by humans. And, as James Madison astutely noted, "If men were angels, no government would be necessary."[8] The inescapable presence of human influence means that many of the theoretical assumptions underlying market interactions are undermined. Markets work best with complete information, for example – that is, accurate information that is freely and equally available to all participants. In the absence of these conditions (i.e., reality), markets become imperfect. The reason why insider trading in shares is illegal is because it directly transgresses on the assumption of complete information.[9] Unfortunately, incomplete or asymmetric information is the norm. Sometimes this is a result of deliberate manipulation (as in the case of insider trading); more often, however, it is due to human limitations (an inability to process large amounts of information, act rationally, ignore sunk costs, evaluate opportunity costs, overcome biases and fears, and so on).[10]

One market that is often cited by supporters as purer than most is the stock market. Yet, we know from prior financial crises that the stock market is inherently challenged when it comes to pricing risk accurately. It is not even clear that investors are good at assessing overall value. As Warren Buffett has stated, "I'd be a bum on the street with a tin cup if the markets were always efficient."[11] The prevalence of bubbles and the tendency toward herd behavior demonstrate that psychology and emotion play as large a part in determining stock movements as rigorous analysis. Buffett's success relies on traders either under- or over-valuing shares as a result of imperfect information and poor judgment, which allows so-called *value traders* to take advantage:

> Mr. Buffett began an investment partnership in 1956 and, over the next 12 years, achieved a 29.5 percent compound return. ... In comparison, the Dow Jones industrial average rose by 7.4 percent per year during the same period. Then, in 1965, Mr. Buffett took control of a small Massachusetts textile manufacturer and through a combination of buying stocks and, later, buying entire companies, achieved a 19.7 percent annual increase in Berkshire Hathaway's stock price while the average was increasing by 9.4 percent.[12]

An example of the limits of the market in valuing goods is evident in relation to nature. Whether dealing with "use value" (natural goods with a functional application, such as water) or "non-use value" (natural goods without a function, but valued for intangible reasons like beauty, such as a water geyser), there are market tools that can be employed (e.g., the level of admission people are willing to pay to visit a national park). Arriving at a complete valuation for such goods, however, is challenging.[13] Fresh water is a good example of this. While it is essential to life and is also relatively scarce (and, therefore, in theory, should have a high valuation), its exchange value is limited (the trade value for a bottle of water is low), largely because equal access to it is considered the cornerstone of a civilized society:

> Adam Smith spotted that economics has problems valuing nature. "Nothing is more useful than water: but it will purchase scarce anything; scarce anything can be had in exchange for it. A diamond, on the contrary, has scarce value in use; but a very great quantity of other goods may frequently be had in exchange for it," he wrote.[14]

The bottled water industry is a good example of how, even when faced with such limitations, the market is able to overcome them – even while the solution provided is replete with additional externalized costs (e.g., increased production of single-use plastics). Similarly, the example of access to clean water demonstrates that, because of the flaws inherent in the application of market ideology, some constraints are often beneficial. As detailed in Principle 4, the ideal in an effective system of checks and balances is empowered and invested stakeholders willing to hold the firm to account. This ensures the firm is incentivized to act in the best interests of its collective set of stakeholders (which, together, constitute society), rather than the interests of a narrow select group, such as its shareholders. Although this perspective implies an equal responsibility across all stakeholders, when CSR advocates envision what such constraints might look like, they tend to focus disproportionately on the role of the government. Of course, there is good reason for this as the government has demonstrated, on many occasions, the value that can be obtained for society by seeking to curb the strongest self-interested impulses of for-profit firms:

> Before the Clean Air Act was passed in 1970 many Americans led shorter, sicker lives because of pollution. White-collar workers in Gary, Indiana, a steel town, often went to work with an extra shirt because the first one looked too dirty by midday. Between 1980 and 2012 total emissions of six common air pollutants in America dropped by 67%, according to the Environmental Protection Agency (EPA). This happened even as the country's population grew by 38% and Americans consumed 27% more energy.[15]

In reality, however, the balance between government oversight and free enterprise is a fine line that politicians often cross, with sub-optimal outcomes. The guiding principle should be to protect the freedom to innovate and conduct commerce, avoid central planning, and curb the greatest excesses of capitalism that result in counter-productive outcomes[16] – "to reconcile the goals of freedom and economic progress, which are paramount in the laissez-faire philosophy, with the goals of stability, security, justice, and personality development, which are emphasized in modern humanitarian philosophy."[17] It is this complex interplay that forms the foundation of modern market capitalism that, via for-profit firms, is the superior structure for allocating resources in ways that promote overall value. In other words, market forces generate better solutions than those arrived at through political distortions, such as coercion (e.g., government regulations), favoritism (e.g., lobbying), price controls (e.g., subsidies or quotas), or nationalist trade protection (e.g., tariffs). The problem with such distortions is that, however well-intentioned, they have a habit of producing unintended consequences that lead to the inefficient allocation of resources and the destruction of value.

Unintended consequences

When market forces are subverted with ulterior goals, unintended consequences are common. At the extreme, the actual consequences achieve the opposite of those that were intended. An example of this might be if an increase in the minimum wage (designed to protect low-wage earners) were to result in a reduction in overall jobs (reducing the number of low-wage jobs available). This effect is based on the assumption that:

> In a competitive market anything that artificially raises the price of labour will curb demand for it, and the first to lose their jobs will be the least skilled – the people intervention is supposed to help. ... [T]opping up the incomes of the working poor with public subsidies [is] a far more sensible means of alleviating poverty.[18]

Economists refer to this phenomenon of unintended consequences as *Jevon's paradox*: "named after a 19th-century British economist who observed that while the steam engine extracted energy more efficiently from coal, it also stimulated so much economic growth that coal consumption increased."[19] A modern update of this example is the unforeseen consequences of energy efficiency, particularly in consumer products, such as appliances or cars. While these innovations undoubtedly use energy more efficiently than the technologies they were designed to replace, there is often a compelling argument that the net energy consumed as a result of their purchase is zero (unchanged) or even positive (an overall increase):

> The problem is known as the energy rebound effect. While there's no doubt that fuel-efficient cars burn less gasoline per mile, the lower cost at the pump tends to encourage extra driving. There's also an indirect rebound effect as drivers use the money they save on gasoline to buy other things that produce greenhouse emissions, like new electronic gadgets or vacation trips on fuel-burning planes.[20]

A related term for this ability to convince ourselves that the best way to solve our excessive resource depletion of the Earth is through further consumption is "The Prius Fallacy."[21] By substituting one (possibly) greener product for another, we kill two birds with one stone – we satisfy both our psychological and material needs. We also give ourselves the *moral license* to continue consuming – a process we are very good at rationalizing after the fact.[22] What we fail to realize is that, even as we innovate and consume, rather than reducing our environmental impact, the unintended consequence is the opposite. While generally ignored by environmentalists today, there are important policy implications to be gleaned from this phenomenon:

> if your immediate goal is to reduce greenhouse emissions, then it seems risky to count on reaching it by improving energy efficiency. To economists worried about rebound effects, it makes more sense to look for new carbon-free sources of energy, or to impose a direct penalty for emissions, like a tax on energy generated from fossil fuels. Whereas people respond to more fuel-efficient cars by driving more and buying other products, they respond to a gasoline tax simply by driving less.[23]

The danger becomes particularly prevalent when artificial economic incentives are added to the consumption equation. For example, during the 18th century, when the British government was still shipping its criminals to Australia, sea captains were compensated based on the number of people they carried on their ships. What the government found, however, was that many inmates were dying during the journey – up to one-third in some instances. Neither taking a doctor onboard for the journey nor raising the captains' compensation increased the number of passengers who survived the trip.

It wasn't until the government began paying captains based on the number of people who arrived in Australia (rather than the number of people who left the UK) that behavior changed and the survival rate greatly increased – to as high as 99%.[24] A similar effect was evident in another example from India:

> During the time of British rule in colonial India, in order to free Delhi from a plague of snakes, the City's governor put an incentive scheme in place for their capture by introducing a bounty on cobra skins. The bounty was quite high as cobras are tricky to catch. And so, instead of the snakes being caught in the city, it became a sound business idea to start farming them. All of a sudden, the number of bounty claims increased disproportionately. The local authority realised what was going on and responded by abandoning the incentive scheme. And as they were no longer profitable, the cobras were released from the farms into the city, exacerbating the original problem.[25]

The key to avoiding such unforeseen consequences is, clearly, to ensure the correct behavior is being incentivized:

> Where governments want to raise revenue without distorting markets, the best approach is to charge businesses a flat fee, like a cab licence. Firms then have an incentive to do as much business as they can. But where governments want to discourage consumption – as with cigarettes and alcohol – they should tax each unit sold.[26]

In the example from India above, the desired outcome was a reduction of the number of snakes in Delhi, but the action that was incentivized was an increase in the number of snakes killed. As demonstrated, these things can result in opposite outcomes in practice. In the case of calls to raise the minimum wage, the goal is to reduce poverty and income disparity, but the action prescribed is to increase the cost of labor. Although economists disagree on the effects of a minimum wage (some research indicates that small increases have little or no effect on job creation), it is possible that in some cases an increase would result in existing employees being fired (because the employer can no longer afford to employ them) or a reduction in the number of new hires (because the cost limits a planned expansion), hence vastly worsening the economic situation for these individuals:

> In flexible economies a low minimum wage seems to have little, if any, depressing effect on employment. America's federal minimum wage, at 38% of median income, is one of the rich world's lowest. Some studies find no harm to employment from federal or state minimum wages, others see a small one, but none finds any serious damage. … High minimum wages, however, particularly in rigid labour markets do appear to hit employment. France has the rich world's highest wage

floor, at more than 60% of the median for adults and a far bigger fraction of the typical wage for the young. This helps explain why France also has shockingly high rates of youth unemployment: 26% for 15- to 24-year olds.[27]

The issue of unintended consequences is one of the most important issues for the CSR community to address, particularly in relation to sustainability. When we attempt to subvert centuries of economic development, substituting altruistic motivation for economic incentives, we should tread carefully. Whether it is government subsidies or tax breaks for a particular kind of alternative energy, or a new technical innovation that interacts with some other factor (or is applied inappropriately), the result is often an unexpected outcome that can detract from, rather than promote, overall value. That is not to say that government intervention is necessarily unwarranted or unhelpful. In fact, in terms of shaping the rules of the game to ensure a level playing field and enforce existing regulations, the government is an essential stakeholder of the firm – what David Sainsbury in his manifesto for *progressive capitalism* refers to as an "enabling state," with responsibilities to support, rather than direct, markets:

> Market institutions are human artefacts created, in all their varieties beyond the most simple, by the state and, ultimately, they all need to be justified by their contribution to the well-being of society and to be perpetually open to reform.[28]

As a general rule, the more heavy-handed or misguided the intervention, the less likely it is to generate an optimal solution. There is still much that we do not understand about the motivations that drive human behavior and generate societal-level outcomes. By definition, we can only base future projections on past experience and are constrained when we do, likely over-emphasizing the potential benefits and failing to account for all risks. That does not mean change should never occur, but it does imply we should be humble in attempts to temper these refined forces that have evolved over centuries. As Adam Smith illustrated in *The Wealth of Nations*:

> The woollen coat, for example, which covers the day-labourer, as coarse and rough as it may appear, is the produce of the joint labour of a multitude of workmen. The shepherd, the sorter of the wool, the wool-comber or carder, the dyer, the scribbler, the spinner, the weaver, the fuller, the dresser, with many others, must all join their different arts in order to complete even this homely production. … Let us consider only what a variety of labour is requisite in order to form that very simple machine, the shears with which the shepherd clips the wool. The miner, the builder of the furnace for smelting the ore, the feller of the timber, the burner of the charcoal to be made use of in the smelting-house, the

brick-maker, the brick-layer, the workmen who attend the furnace, the mill-wright, the forger, the smith. … Without the assistance and co-operation of many thousands, the very meanest person in a civilized country could not be provided, even according to what we very falsely imagine, the easy and simple manner in which he is commonly accommodated.[29]

As Smith insightfully demonstrates, it is the effect of hundreds of individuals, each pursuing their individual interests, that collectively ensure the laborer's coat is made in a way that meets the laborer's needs. Moreover, the pursuit of self-interest is not devoid of morals or ethics. On the contrary, as Adam Gopnik explains in his summary of Adam Smith's work, a framework of guiding values is inherently embedded in the application of market forces:

Where can you find a sympathetic community, people working in uncanny harmony, each aware of the desires of the other and responding to them with grace and reciprocal charm? Forget the shepherds in Arcadia. Ignore the poets in Parnassus. Visit a mall. For Smith the plain-seeing Scot, the market may not be the most elegant instance of human sympathy, but it's the most insistent: everybody has skin in the game. … That's what keeps the mob from rushing the Victoria's Secret and stealing knives from the Hoffritz and looting the Gap. Shopping, which for the church moralist is a straight path to sin, is for Smith a shortcut to sympathy. Money is the surest medium of exchange.[30]

The phenomenon of *Jevons paradox* demonstrates that good intentions that seek to subvert market forces and established market practices can result in counter-productive outcomes. Markets are far from perfect and can distort behavior, but manufactured interventions exacerbate this possibility. As such, the conflicting stakeholder interests described in Principle 4 demonstrate the value in encouraging checks and balances that can curb the market's worst excesses. Government regulation is one of these checks, but should be applied cautiously. The ideal would be to design more intelligent curbs that avoid unforeseen consequences by accounting for what we know of the imperfections involved in implementing market ideology (i.e., by accounting for human behavior).

Behavioral economics

In 2002, the psychologist Daniel Kahneman won the Nobel Prize for Economics for his work on the cognitive biases of humans. In his 2011 book, *Thinking, Fast and Slow*,[31] he notes that the human brain works with two systems – one that helps make decisions rapidly based on emotion ("fast thinking"), while a second helps make decisions more deliberately ("slow thinking"), but often rationalizes the choices generated by the first system.

The combination creates a contrast between the rational, agentic decision-makers that we think we are and the emotional, impulsive decision-makers that the evidence suggests we are more often:

> Although humans are not irrational, they often need help to make more accurate judgments and better decisions, and in some cases policies and institutions can provide that help. ... The assumption that agents are rational provides the intellectual foundation for the libertarian approach to public policy: do not interfere with the individual's right to choose, unless the choices harm others. ... For behavioral economists, however, freedom has a cost, which is borne by individuals who make bad choices, and by a society that feels obligated to help them.[32]

Many of these ideas, which integrate insights from economics and psychology (social and cognitive), form the foundation of what today is known as behavioral (or *nudge*)[33] economics. The advantage of behavioral economics is that it works with what we know of the imperfections in human nature to curb the raw excesses of market forces, yet preserves the illusion of choice that markets enable and is an essential component of an open society:

> Behavioural economists have found that all sorts of psychological or neurological biases cause people to make choices that seem contrary to their best interests. The idea of nudging is based on research that shows it is possible to steer people towards better decisions by presenting choices in different ways.[34]

If there was wider use of behavioral economics in policy making, it is argued, we would be able to nudge individuals to make decisions that better serve their own (and society's) interests. When deployed intelligently, the results can be powerful:

> In one trial, a letter sent to non-payers of vehicle taxes was changed to use plainer English, along the line of "pay your tax or lose your car". In some cases the letter was further personalised by including a photo of the car in question. The rewritten letter alone doubled the number of people paying the tax; the rewrite with the photo tripled it. ... A study into the teaching of technical drawing in French schools found that if the subject was called "geometry" boys did better, but if it was called "drawing" girls did equally well or better. Teachers are now being trained to use the appropriate term.[35]

Nudge economics demonstrates the value of an accurate, grounded appreciation of human nature – explaining behavior due to empirical observation rather than ideological assumption. The results, when implemented, demonstrate how human decision-making can be shaped dramatically by applying this knowledge to public policy (and, by extension, to market interactions):

When you renew your driver's license, you have a chance to enroll in an organ donation program. In countries like Germany and the U.S., you have to check a box if you want to opt in. Roughly 14 percent of people do. But behavioral scientists have discovered that how you set the defaults is really important. So in other countries, like Poland or France, you have to check a box if you want to opt out. In these countries, more than 90 percent of people participate.[36]

It is fascinating how relatively simple incentive structures can be used to nudge people in the direction of greater societal value. One more example presents the dramatic shifts in eating behavior among children achieved through subtle changes to the layouts of school cafeterias:

> A smarter lunchroom wouldn't be draconian. Rather, it would nudge students toward making better choices on their own by changing the way their options are presented. One school we have observed in upstate New York, for instance, tripled the number of salads students bought simply by moving the salad bar away from the wall and placing it in front of the cash registers.[37]

In considering the value of behavioral economics for *Sustainable Value Creation (SVC)*, it is important to think through two considerations. On the one hand, what rights do consumers have to purchase resource-intensive products, even if we assume that the full costs associated with producing that product (i.e., all externalities) are incorporated into its purchase price? Should we have the right to destroy the environment if that is the result of the decisions we make (consciously or unconsciously)? On the other hand, what role should the government play in micro-managing our lives, given the blunt tools it uses to decide where to draw the lines, as well as the biased and corrupt process by which it does so (due to the influence of money in determining which lines at which times)? The debate between the value of a strong, benevolent government that can shape a progressive society (in theory) and the inefficiency and unintended outcomes associated with top-down directives (in reality) is extremely difficult to resolve:

> Milton Friedman didn't need behavioral economics to know that each of us typically spends our own money on ourselves more wisely than a stranger spends other people's money on us.[38]

My first instinct was to agree with this quote. After all, government has consistently demonstrated an inability to shape outcomes as effectively as markets. On second thoughts, however, it is clear we are often incapable of making ideal (or even beneficial) decisions when left to our own intuition. Because humans are driven by our inherent and persistent fallibilities (bounded rationality, innate biases, emotional impulses, and cognitive constraints), we often make short-term decisions that do not serve our long-term interests. This happens even when we are trying to be rational – there are good reasons, for example, why many people fail to save enough money for their retirement, even when they have the capacity (sufficient earnings) and tools (corporate pension plans) to do so.

Given that we are living in a system designed for and operated by humans, where is the balance between government oversight and individual enterprise? As an integral component of *SVC*, behavioral economics helps push the debate in a helpful direction. Cass Sunstein, who wrote *Nudge* with Richard Thaler,[39] for example, draws on human frailties, such as "'framing effects' (our interpretation of facts is affected by how they are presented to us) and 'status-quo bias' (we prefer the status quo, simply because it is the status quo, over potential alternatives) to promote what he calls 'libertarian paternalism'":[40]

> Government, he thinks, should change behavior using "nudges" instead of commands. Regulations can tap into people's psychological quirks and prompt them to choose "better" behaviors – while still leaving them free in many circumstances to act differently. Cigarette packages with grisly images of cancer-ridden lungs are an effort to nudge – rather than command – people not to smoke.[41]

It is important to tread carefully here. There is a reason why the market economy has proved so resilient – it draws on core human values and desires and accounts for them in a way that, in general, optimizes outcomes. And, if anything, we are inertial, captive to patterns and biases that are deeply ingrained in all of us. As Bill Frederick reminds us,

> what we are today is, to a very large extent, a function of what we were yesterday. … this means [for business practitioners] that there is not likely to be any escape from the very powerful motive of private gain and profit, which is often at variance with social interest.[42]

In other words, it is more effective to work within the constraints of human nature as it is, rather than as we would wish it to be. Behavioral economics does this by incorporating aspects of social and cognitive psychology into economic models that would otherwise rely on unrealistic assumptions about human behavior. As the noted economist, N. Gregory Mankiw, admits:

> We economists often have only a basic understanding of how most policies work. The economy is complex and economic science is still a primitive body of knowledge. Because unintended consequences are the norm, what seems like a utility-maximizing policy can often backfire. … In some ways, economics is like medicine two centuries ago. If you were ill at the beginning of the 19th century, a physician was your best bet,

but his knowledge was so rudimentary that his remedies could easily make things worse rather than better. And so it is with economics today.[43]

Nudge economics incorporates the biases and prejudices that inform our decisions into policies that encourage *optimal* social outcomes, while still retaining the *illusion* of choice. As such, it is a valuable consideration in the debate between government oversight and unrestricted market forces and, therefore, is an important part of *SVC*.

Summary

Principle 5 states that *Market-based solutions are optimal*. It argues that, while markets are far from perfect, they are the most efficient means we have of allocating scarce and valuable resources via the for-profit firms that populate them. More importantly, the evidence suggests that, when we seek to subvert these highly developed forces, however well-intentioned, the result is often an unintended consequence that destroys (rather than creates) value. One way to curb the raw excesses of market forces, yet preserve the illusion of choice that markets enable, is the wider use of behavioral economics to help *nudge* individuals to make decisions that better serve their own (and society's) interests.

Principle 6

Profit = total value

Key takeaway: In essence, a firm's profit represents the ability to sell a good or service at a higher price than what it costs to produce. Production and consumption, however, are more than merely technical decisions. They encapsulate the total value (to all stakeholders) that is added by the firm.

A significant reason for the supremacy of market forces in delivering value to stakeholders, as discussed in Principle 5, is the pivotal role played by profit:

> The existence of a profit is an indication *prima facie* that the business has succeeded in producing something which consumers want and value. ... a business that fails to make an adequate profit is a house of cards. It cannot grow or provide more jobs or pay higher wages. In the long run, it cannot even survive. It offers no stability or security or opportunity for its workers and investors. It cannot meet its broader obligations to society. It is a failure from all points of view.[1]

I would amend this quote only to replace the narrow stakeholder group, *consumers*, with the much broader concept of *society*. If a society (the collective set of all stakeholders) permits a firm to continue operations, then it is acknowledging that it adds value – that society is better off than if the firm did not exist. At present, the best method we have of measuring that value is the profit the firm generates. This statement is core to the idea of *Sustainable Value Creation* (*SVC*), but exists in contrast to the way profit is often discussed within the CSR community – as a narrow measure of economic value and something that can detract from social, moral, and ethical value. This representation of *economic value* as an independent construct, separate from other kinds of value, demonstrates a misunderstanding of what profit is and how it is generated. In reality, a firm's profit represents the total value added, to all stakeholders, as a result of ongoing operations.

Economic value + social value

The profit motive is closely linked in business to the price mechanism, which is an assessment of the cost of bringing a product or service to market, plus a margin that provides sufficient incentive for the business to operate. In the marketplace, *price* is the best way we have developed to measure the value-added in an exchange. In terms of firm performance, a profit or loss is the aggregated outcome of multiple production and consumption decisions. These decisions are arrived at through individual evaluations of cost and benefit along many, many dimensions, at each stage of development, and ultimately expressed in the consumer's willingness to pay the price that is being charged. If the value I obtain from a product exceeds the costs involved in earning sufficient money to pay the price, then I should be willing to buy it. In other words, when I buy a product, I am signaling to the firm that I value what it does. When this transaction is repeated by all stakeholders in each of the ways they interact with the firm, this signal amounts to a societal-wide sanction of the underlying business. As Howard Bowen noted back in 1953:

> when businessmen follow the profit motive they are merely following social valuations as expressed in the prices at which they can sell their products and the prices at which they can buy productive services, materials, supplies, and their other requirements. ... When the businessman follows this signal, he is following not only his own interest but that of society as well. ... The practical and the democratic thing for him to do is to rely primarily on profit as his guide in deciding his business actions.[2]

Conceptually, therefore, while it can be helpful to think of *economic value* and *social value* as separate constructs; in reality, they are not independent. On the contrary, they are highly correlated and infused in the firm's decisions regarding production (Do we pollute the local river or not? Do we hire at the minimum wage or a living wage?) and the consumer's decisions regarding consumption (Do I buy from the firm that produces locally or the one that outsources? Do I pay the premium associated with a more environmentally friendly product or purchase the cheaper, disposable product?). Further, they are embedded in all stakeholders' decisions to interact with the firm. All of these production and consumption decisions contain value-laden foundations and consequences that, ultimately, sum to determine the economic success of the firm:

> Two hundred years' worth of work in economics and finance indicate that social welfare is maximized when all firms in an economy maximize total firm value. The intuition behind this criterion is simply that (social) value is created when a firm produces an output or set of outputs that are valued by its customers at more than the value of the inputs it consumes (as valued by their suppliers) in such production. Firm value is simply the long-term market value of this stream of benefits.[3]

Similarly, we know from a significant body of research in fields such as strategy and marketing that, when I buy a product, I am not just purchasing something that will fulfill a technical function – I am buying something that makes me happy, that conveys my status, that boosts my self-esteem, and, yes, something that is *socially responsible* (depending on the values I hold and the criteria I prioritize in my purchase decisions). This is something that we all know intuitively to be true. It is why car companies like BMW, Mercedes, and Audi exist – they provide a product that does much more for the consumer than transport them from point A to point B.

In addition to this private, non-technical value that is built into the price the consumer pays for a good, there is also a component that relates to the level of public value that is generated. If I buy a Toyota Prius, for example, I pay a premium over similar, non-hybrid cars because of the superior technology built into the Prius' engine and battery. While I get a private benefit from this purchase in that I can now demonstrate to everyone how environmentally conscious I am, there is also a significant public benefit in the reduced pollution that my car emits. In this, the price I am paying represents a partial subsidy to society in that I am covering the cost of improving the air quality, incrementally – a positive externality from which everyone benefits, but is built into the price that I pay (and, therefore, is incorporated into the profit that Toyota reports at the end of the year). More specifically, by providing this product that reduces environmental pollution, is Toyota engaged in solving an economic problem (the demand for cars) or a social problem (the need to transport people in a way that minimizes damage to the environment)?

Management researchers talk about the need for "compassion in organizations" that allows them also to "focus on social problems and social welfare concerns,"[4] as if economic problems and social problems are separate entities. Again, a simple thought experiment highlights the overly-simplistic nature of this forced dichotomy. Is feeding people a social problem or an economic problem? Of course, there are hundreds of for-profit food manufacturers (not to mention the hundreds of thousands of restaurants and supermarkets) that produce food and distribute it widely (and efficiently) to whole populations of people. What about clothing people – a social problem or an economic problem? A visit to the mall will quickly reveal how efficiently for-profit firms have essentially eradicated the supply of clothes as a challenge for all but the most deprived societies. Or, what about providing internet access to every household in the country – economic or social? Certainly, you could make an argument that, today, a family is essentially excluded from many aspects of society if it cannot get online ("what many people consider as basic a utility as water and electricity");[5] yet, internet provision in most developed economies is the sole responsibility of the private sector (as it is for the food and apparel industries).

So, how is it that for-profit firms are not already intricately involved in addressing social problems? In fact, you could argue that, essentially, every company uses economic means to solve social problems. Now, you may challenge the business models of some of these firms, or the quality of the final product they produce, but I believe there is no way that anyone can say these for-profit firms are not involved in addressing complex problems that have intertwined economic and social (and moral and ethical) components. In essence, there are no economic problems or social problems; there are just *problems* that have both social and economic consequences.

As the above examples indicate, much of what is referred to as *social value* (the value that is derived above and beyond the functional purpose of a product or service) is largely captured in a willingness among consumers to part with their disposable income. Given that, for most of us, our disposable income is a scarce resource, how we decide to spend it reflects our values in action. That is not to say that market forces are perfect, as noted in Principle 5. Unfortunately, 100% of social value is not captured in the price charged and the profit earned. Negative externalities are a good example of how imperfect the market can be (e.g., pollution during manufacturing that goes undetected, or the pollution involved during consumption that is not paid for). Human beings' tendency to favor short-term gratification over longer-term investments (which explains why many people fail to save sufficient funds for their retirement) is another example of how the private profits that are generated immediately as a result of our consumption decisions do not reflect perfectly the public costs incurred by society at some later date:

> The profit motive can be objected to legitimately when the quest for profits results in restrictive monopoly, exploitation, fraud, misrepresentation, political bribery, waste of nature resources, economic insecurity, etc. It is the *abuse* of the profit motive, not the motive itself, that comes under criticism.[6]

Nevertheless, given what we know, monetary value is the best way we have of capturing overall value creation. The price of a product and the profit of a firm incorporate a significant amount of all aspects of value (economic, social, moral, and ethical) that is encapsulated in market transactions. While the correlation among these different measures of value is high, however, it is not perfect. As such, *SVC* exists to redefine our understanding of economic exchange in order to minimize the gap among different measures of value. One example of this is to ensure that firms internalize the complete costs of production and consumption in the price that is charged for the finished good (detailed in Principle 7). Before we turn to that discussion, however, it is necessary to complete our consideration of the role played by profit in terms of total value creation.

Profit optimization

In the process of delivering value to its broad range of stakeholders, it is essential that the firm generates a profit. Profit generation is, therefore, also central to the concept of *SVC*. Rather than challenge what the firm does (make money), *SVC* is focused more specifically on how the firm does it (the hundreds and thousands of operational decisions made every day). In the process, one of the goals of *SVC* is to shift the debate around the purpose of the for-profit firm in society. By challenging taken-for-granted assumptions about business and the value it delivers, the potential for reform to help build a more sustainable economic system becomes possible. One of the taken-for-granted assumptions that must be challenged is the idea that firms pursue policies and practices that result in *profit maximization*. First, this concept is not provable; second, it is unhelpful.

First, the idea of profit maximization is something that is impossible to prove as a firm can never know whether the profit generated was in fact maximized or what effect making an alternative decision would have had instead:

> A simple statement that managers try to maximize corporate profits, as is frequently assumed in economic theory, is almost meaningless. The concept of profit is a highly tenuous one in that it involves the valuation of assets, the allocation of joint costs, the treatment of developmental expenses, and a host of similar problems for which there are no easy or definite solutions. The idea of profit maximization raises the troublesome question of the time period over which profits are to be maximized, and it is difficult for either managers or observers to calculate the effect on profits of given actions which may affect the business indefinitely in the future. Obviously, businessmen [sic] are often deterred by custom and by ethical principle from exacting the highest possible profit. The businessman may forgo profits to avoid the demands of organized labor, or public regulation, or entry of new firms. Businessmen often show greater interest in business volume and business expansion that they do in profits. … It may be more realistic to describe the quest for profit as a seeking for "satisfactory profits" rather than maximum profits ("satisfactory" defined in relation to the profit experience of other firms).[7]

Second, the idea of profit maximization is unhelpful. It is an ideological fallacy that distorts expectations and decision-making within the firm. The only way we can know if a particular set of decisions maximized profits for the firm is to re-run the time period, under the exact same internal and external conditions, investigating all the different possible combinations of decision outcomes. Given that there is no control group,[8] it is not possible to know whether current profits are any higher or lower than if different decisions had been made. As such, the decision matrix that guides the firm comes down to a debate among different philosophies – for example, Do you believe paying a minimum wage to employees will generate larger profits (by reducing costs) than will be generated by paying a living wage (by increasing loyalty and productivity)? Any firm or executive that claims their set of decisions *maximize* profits for the firm is, therefore, being disingenuous at best; most likely, they do not fully understand the nature of the statement and certainly cannot in any way prove the claim. As Robert Skidelsky reminds us:

> Economics is luxuriant with fallacies, because it is not a natural science like physics or chemistry. Propositions in economics are rarely absolutely true or false. What is true in some circumstances may be false in others. Above all, the truth of many propositions depends on people's expectations.[9]

As a result of being both impossible to achieve and unhelpful because it distorts decision-making, rather than profit *maximization*, a more valuable focus for firms to adopt is the goal of profit *optimization*. Although equally impossible to prove definitively, profit optimization (rather than maximization) is a flexible goal that more closely approximates the subjective nature of the decision-making process – different people will use different sets of values to determine what they consider to be *optimal*. In other words, while the idea of a *maximum* suggests an absolute point (a definitive highest amount), an *optimum* suggests a more relative state of existence. What is optimal for me may not be optimal for you, but you cannot say the values by which I determine my optimum are wrong, just that they differ from the values you use to determine your optimum. As such, this rhetorical shift helps encourage a balance between short-, medium-, and long-term decisions that create value across the firm's broad range of stakeholders.

Production value and consumption value

As the discussion above indicates, while defining social value and economic value and understanding how they relate to each other appears superficially straightforward, it is highly complex in reality. Beyond a conceptual discussion, it is also useful to think through the challenges of drawing this distinction in practice. For example: Do employees' wages relate to economic value (a cost of production) or social value (a determinant of income inequality)? Similarly, is the level of pollution related to economic value (an output of production) or social value (a blight that is borne by society)? In both cases, you might answer "both" and, of course, you would be correct. In reality, there is no *social value* and no *economic value*; there is only *value* (positive and negative) that is distributed among all stakeholders in different ways due to different decisions. Any attempt to present these highly complex and complementary concepts as independent reveals a fundamental misunderstanding of the role firms play in society, but also of the ability of profit to capture what people mean when they talk about social (and ethical and moral) value.

Given these complexities, an alternative conceptualization is to think of the value added by a firm during production and the value added by a product or service during consumption. At either stage, the assessment of the value added would be either neutral, net positive, or net negative. In this alternative conceptualization, employees' wages would contribute to the total value added during production, as would any pollution emitted during manu-facturing, while pollution emitted during consumption (e.g., driving a car, the e-waste created by a discarded smartphone) would be accounted for as part of the value added (or subtracted) during consumption. The net effect, in theory, would define our collective quality of life and, in turn, help deter-mine necessary reforms:

> Our standard of living ... consists of two parts: that which derives from the conditions under which production is carried on and that which derives from the goods and services resulting from that production. An improvement in the conditions of production – resulting in a better working environment of better functioning of the economy – may fre-quently be entirely justified even if achieved at a sacrifice in output of final goods and services.[10]

The challenge we face as a society, therefore, is to strike a balance between the part of our standard of living that is formed from the production of goods and services, and the part of our standard of living that is formed from the consumption of those goods and services. The production component includes incorporating costs that firms currently seek to externalize (such as the pollution emitted during manufacturing), while the consumption com-ponent includes incorporating costs that society currently seeks to avoid (such as the pollution emitted during consumption, e.g., driving a car or discarding e-waste). If a marginal $1 spent on production yields greater returns than the same $1 spent on consumption, it is in our collective best interests to spend the $1 on improving aspects of production (and vice-versa). While true, it is also important to keep in mind that understanding the true nature of what profit represents is conceptually important, but helpful only up to a point. If we accept that long-term profit is a good (if imperfect) measure of total value added, we must also recognize that it is just that – a measure of performance that still does not help us understand how the firm should go about adding that value:

> Defining what it means to score a goal in football or soccer, for example, tells the players nothing about how to win the game. It just tells them how the score will be kept. That is the role of value maximization in organizational life.[11]

In other words, profit is the outcome of a highly complex process that, more accurately, determines whether the firm is being *socially responsible*. As such, it is the detail of that complex process that matters. Understanding how firms can balance the pursuit of profit and the need to satisfy a broad range of stakeholder interests (how they should achieve their profit) is essential.

Recognizing that this realization of empowered stakeholders is achieved largely through the value creation process, and that a necessary element of this is understanding what *value* (all kinds of value) looks like for each of these stakeholders, is central to understanding the different approach to business that is demanded by *SVC*.

Summary

Principle 6 states that *Profit = total value*. It argues that conceptualizing economic value as an independent construct, separate from other kinds of value (such as social, ethical, and moral), demonstrates a fundamental misunderstanding of what profit represents. Although imperfect, profit is the best measure we have of capturing the total value added by a specific company and product/service during production and consumption. Rather than asking firms to focus on *profit maximization* (both impossible to prove and unhelpful because it distorts decision-making), the goal of *profit optimization* better reflects the value judgments made every day as firms balance competing stakeholder interests. Even better, understanding the total value added in terms of the separate processes associated with production and consumption provides a mechanism by which society can more easily identify those behaviors that create (and destroy) total value.

Principle 7

The *free* market is not free

Key takeaway: The free market is an illusion. It encourages firms to externalize costs that are borne by society rather than consumers; it is rife with subsidies
and quotas that favor some firms and industries over others. The result is an
economic system that is distorted and, as a result, unsustainable.

As explored in Principle 6, although economic value and social value are
highly correlated, the relationship is not perfect. In other words, not all of the
value that is sought by stakeholders is captured in the profit generated by the
firm. The reason for this is that our current economic model is distorted. In
order to build on Principles 5 and 6, therefore, it is essential to address the
structural characteristics that embed barriers to free exchange throughout the
economy.

In terms of protectionism, for example, the barriers to trade are numerous
and, because they are often designed to appease local political constituencies,
can appear absurd from afar. America, for example, reportedly "tacks a 127%
tariff on to Chinese paper clips,"[1] while Japan continues to levy "a whopping
778% tariff on imported rice."[2] Amazingly, $500 billion is spent by govern-
ments worldwide on energy subsidies, "the equivalent of four times all official
foreign aid."[3] And, when externalized costs are added to these subsidies, the
IMF estimates that "the fossil fuel industry got a whopping $5.2 trillion in
subsidies in 2017. This amounts to 6.4 percent of the global gross domestic
product."[4] For these reasons (and many more – quotas, tax breaks, bailouts,
export rebates, externalities, and so on), markets are far from freely competitive. Failed oversight and misaligned incentives allow otherwise uncompetitive firms and harmful products to remain viable, while active
intervention, usually by the government, undermines innovation and free
enterprise.[5] Overall, the wide variety of market distortions generate an economic system that is less efficient, less competitive, and less sustainable than it
otherwise would be.[6]

Free markets

As currently constituted, "markets fail to price the true costs of goods."[7] The reason for this is that the markets we have created are riddled with inefficiencies (what politicians call subsidies, tax breaks, legal loopholes, etc.). These inefficiencies introduce costs into the system and skew incentives that, together, sustain uncompetitive companies and erect barriers to more competitive alternatives. As such, we need to reform our market system. The goal should be to work toward a model in which all costs are included in the price charged for each product and service. An economy where externalities are internalized and embedded within a moral framework moves us closer to the economy Adam Smith envisioned and wrote about in his classic treatise *The Theory of Moral Sentiments*[8] – truly free markets filled with values-based businesses and vigilant, engaged stakeholders. Instead in the U.S., for example, we have a very different reality:

> Every year, states and local governments give economic-development incentives to companies to the tune of between $45 billion and $80 billion. Why such a wide range? It's not sloppy research; it's because many of these subsidies are not public. For the known subsidies, such as Maryland's recent $8.5 billion incentive bid for Amazon's second headquarters, the support includes cash grants for company relocations, subsidized land, forgiving company taxes on everything from property taxes to sales taxes and investments in infrastructure for the company. Maryland is even offering to give [the state income tax rate of] 5.75 percent of each worker's salary back to the company.[9]

Politicians on both the left and the right tend to favor government intervention when it is in support of a cause in which they believe (e.g., subsidies for solar power on the left; tax breaks for oil firms on the right), but at least the left admits that it favors government intervention. Right-wing ideology, in contrast, preaches free market ideas, but then implements heavily subsidized intervention in contravention of that ideology. Although shocking in itself, the above quote about the extent of corporate welfare only hints at the inefficient system of corporate support we have created in the West. A good example of these distortions can be found in the energy market:

> Economics 101 tells us that an industry imposing large costs on third parties should be required to "internalize" those costs. ... [Energy extraction by] Fracking might still be worth doing given those costs. But no industry should be held harmless from its impacts on the environment and the nation's infrastructure. Yet what the industry and its defenders demand is, of course, precisely that it be let off the hook for the damage it causes. Why? Because we need that energy![10]

In a similar way, a significant cost associated with nuclear energy is absorbed by the government when it takes responsibility for waste containment. While there is a valid national security interest in doing so, the effect is to externalize the true cost of nuclear power generation. A truly *free* market is only possible, therefore, if we both reduce government intervention (i.e., the removal of subsidies, quotas, tax breaks, etc.) *and* internalize all externalities in pricing. One without the other is not *free*; at present, we have neither:

> So it's worth pointing out that special treatment for fracking makes a mockery of free-market principles. Pro-fracking politicians claim to be against subsidies, yet letting an industry impose costs without paying compensation is in effect a huge subsidy. They say they oppose having the government "pick winners," yet they demand special treatment for this industry precisely because they claim it will be a winner.[11]

In this light, a government tax on carbon is simply a means of accounting for the full environmental costs of oil/gas extraction, processing, and consumption. In other words, it is a means of creating the conditions for a *free* market. Once the level playing field has been created (with more accurate prices for all forms of energy), then the market will determine which energy sources should drive our future economies. Ultimately:

> markets are truly free only when everyone pays the full price for his or her actions. Anything else is socialism. ... Our future will largely be determined by our ability to admit the need to end planetary socialism. That's the most fundamental of economics lessons and one any serious environmentalist ought to heed.[12]

Externalities

A core tenet of economic theory is that, over the long run, prices are formed by the market in response to demand and supply and, as such, are essentially outside the control of individual firms. In other words, in the long run, firms can only charge what market forces will allow them to charge. Any higher and the firm will lose business to its competitors; any lower and the firm will, at a minimum, leave money on the table and, more likely, will operate at a loss.

The problem with this theory is twofold: first, many of the assumptions that accompany it (free and open competition, complete information, equal access among buyers and sellers, etc.) are rarely, if ever, present; and second, most business occurs in the short run – as Keynes noted, "In the long run we are all dead."[13] As a result, markets are imperfect and prices fail to capture all costs associated with production and consumption. Given the opportunity, firms will externalize these costs, allowing others (society, broadly speaking) to incur them. Thus, firms are not directly responsible for building roads, although they benefit greatly from using them to transport goods; they also do not pay for the education system, legal infrastructure, or national defense, even though they value access to an educated workforce, enforceable property rights, and stable borders. All of these costs are what economists refer to as an *externality* – a cost (or benefit) that is incurred, but not paid for, either by the firm (during production) or the purchaser (during consumption):

> Over the past century, companies have been rewarded financially for maximizing externalities in order to minimize costs. ... Not until we more broadly "price in" the external costs of investment decision across all sectors will we have a sustainable economy and society.[14]

While it takes 500–2,000 liters of water to produce the 4oz. of ginned cotton necessary to make a cotton T-shirt, for example, the farmer who produced that 4oz. of cotton receives only approximately U.S.$0.20.[15] This is because, in many countries, water is provided free or heavily subsidized by the state in ways that fail to reflect either the true value of water in the production process or the cost of replenishing stocks so others may have a guaranteed supply in the future. Clearly this is less than optimal because it distorts the normal interaction of demand and supply to create an artificially low price (and distorted market) for, in this case, T-shirts. If we are to fundamentally reform our economic model, therefore, a vital step is to account adequately for such externalities. In other words, the price of a product should not only include the cost of production, but also the cost of replenishing the raw material and disposing/recycling the waste post-consumption. If all firms are forced to incorporate externalities into the price of the finished product or service, many of the cheap items in our disposable economy will become significantly more expensive and firms will be incentivized to produce sustainable alternatives.

Lifecycle pricing

A major flaw in economic theory will remain if we continue to allow resources to be treated as though they are infinite. Until Elon Musk works out a way to get us to Mars,[16] there is only one planet and, as much research has demonstrated, we are already placing significant constraints on the resources at our disposal:

> Some seven billion people are alive today; the United Nations estimates that by the end of the century we could number as many as 15.8 billion. Biologists have calculated that an ideal population – the number at which everyone could live at a first-world level of consumption, without ruining the planet irretrievably – would be 1.5 billion. ... Each year the world adds the equivalent of another Germany or Egypt; by 2040, China will have more than 100 million 80-year-olds. We add another million people every four and a half days.[17]

Population level, in itself, however, is not necessarily a problem. It is a large population combined with a materialistic lifestyle that places such a strain on resource levels:

> If everyone on Earth lived the lifestyle of a traditional Indian villager, it is arguable that even 12 billion would be a sustainable world population. If everyone lives like an upper-middle-class North American (a status to which much of the world seems to aspire), then even two billion is unsustainable.[18]

There is a cost to extraction, production, and consumption without reuse or replenishment.[19] Waste, wherever it occurs in the value chain, is a significant economic and ecological drag on efficiency.[20] Externalities distort markets and underprice products that generate long-term ecological damage. Where resources can be re-used or replenished, we need to account for the cost of doing so in the prices charged to consumers. Where resources cannot be re-used or replenished, we need to impose a cost that accounts for the permanent loss to humanity that results from their extraction. As Paul Hawken astutely put it:

> Without doubt, the single most damaging aspect of the present economic system is that the expense of destroying the earth is largely absent from the prices set in the marketplace.[21]

One idea that has been proposed to solve the problem of externalities by accounting for (internalizing) these true costs is *lifecycle pricing*[22] (related to the idea of *Pigovian taxes*).[23] In other words, the price of a product should not only include the cost of production, but also include the costs associated with replenishing the raw materials used and disposing/recycling of the waste after consumption.[24] Attempts to price carbon reflect this process (either through a carbon tax or some form of cap-and-trade), while firms' efforts to measure the carbon footprints of their products (such as a carton of Tropicana orange juice)[25] provide a possible means of implementation.

The core idea behind lifecycle pricing is to capture all of the impacts at each step of the production process and assign a quantitative value to that step. At the risk of over-simplifying a highly complex calculation (managing to avoid double-counting is, in itself, extremely challenging); in essence, lifecycle pricing requires a firm to add up all the positive and negative costs in the value chain to arrive at a net impact score for each product. This is important because, "If prices reflected all the costs, including ecological costs spread across generations, the world would not face sustainability challenges; at least in theory."[26] The debate surrounding the pricing of "natural capital" (the resources that exist naturally and are exploited by business, often for free – a form of "environmental profit and loss accounting")[27] is central to this task:

Natural capital is simple. The value of well-functioning natural systems is clearly manifest to all people and companies – in the form of clean air, reliable availability of freshwater and productive topsoil in which to grow food, among other benefits. Yet, the way that finance works – from GDP calculations through corporate to accounting – it is as if reliable flows from well-functioning natural systems have no value.[28]

One of the earliest adopters of the concept of "environmental profit and loss" (EP&L) accounting was Puma. The firm developed and first published an EP&L statement in 2011, in which it concluded its operations had an "impact of €51 million resulting from land use, air pollution and waste along the value chain added to previously announced €94 million for GHG emissions and water consumption."[29] It is an idea that is making progress, with a number of firms already incorporating carbon pricing into their planning and budgeting models. Sometimes this is driven by a genuine desire to account for all costs incurred; other times it is to prepare for anticipated legislation that must come at some point. Exxon, for example, applies a cost of "$80 a tonne … when making investment decisions for 10 years,"[30] while Microsoft "charges all departments for every kilowatt-hour of dirty energy they contract or air mile flown by executives, to help meet firm–wide climate targets."[31] According to CDP, "a British watchdog, 607 [firms] now claim to use 'internal carbon prices.' … Another 782 companies say they will introduce similar measures within two years."[32]

If firms can account for all costs incurred at all stages of the value chain (extraction, processing, manufacture, wholesale/retail, purchase/consumption, disposal/recycling), including transportation and storage, as well as all resource inputs (e.g., energy and materials) and outputs (e.g., waste and other pollutants), they would have an accurate snapshot of the true costs involved in producing a product. More important, they would be able to include those costs in the price they charge to customers, which would then allow the market to determine the true demand for that product. Perhaps the best example of a firm that has comprehensively attempted to integrate this life-cycle approach throughout all aspects of operations is Interface carpets, whose inspirational founder and CEO, the late Ray Anderson, explained his journey in terms of the seven (+1) faces of *Mount Sustainability*: 1. Waste. 2. Emissions. 3. Energy. 4. Materials. 5. Transportation. 6. Culture. 7. Market. 8. Social equity.[33] In Anderson's vision, the peak of the mountain represents *sustainability*, which he defines as "take nothing, do no harm." The natural conclusion of such a closed-loop system is zero waste and, to Anderson, this makes perfect business sense:

> More happiness with less stuff. You know, that would reframe civilization itself and our whole system of economics – if not for our species, then perhaps for the one that succeeds us – the sustainable species, living on a finite earth, ethically, happily, and ecologically in balance with

nature and all her natural systems for a thousand generations or ten thousand generations. ... But, does the Earth have to wait for our extinction as a species ... I don't think so. At Interface, we really intend to bring this prototypical, sustainable, zero-footprint industrial company fully into existence by 2020. We can see our way now clear to the top of that mountain and now the challenge is in execution.[34]

It is only by developing industry-wide standards within a lifecycle pricing model that we will move closer to understanding the holistic impact of our current economic system and business practices.[35] We have created an economy based on convenience and waste – we spend money we do not have, on things we do not want, for purposes that are often unimportant.[36] To begin to rectify this, we need to find a way to decrease our unsustainable exploitation of virgin resources. The market remains the most effective means we have of allocating scarce and valuable resources in ways that optimize social outcomes. Rather than continue to subsidize specific industries and uncompetitive firms, lifecycle pricing allows for a less distorted competition of ideas in the marketplace that should also generate more sustainable (and socially responsible) outcomes.

Summary

Principle 7 states that *The* free *market is not free*. It argues that, at present, our economic system allows firms to externalize costs (to society) that are then not included in the prices that are charged (to customers). The problem, therefore, is not that the price mechanism does not work, but that all relevant costs are not currently included in the prices that are charged. And if prices are distorted, the resulting economic exchange will be distorted – producers benefit from lower costs, while consumers benefit from lower prices, and the rest of us pick up the tab. Not only does this create an artificial market for existing products and services; it creates artificial barriers to entry for more competitive alternatives. The solution lies in *lifecycle pricing*, where all related costs of production and consumption are incorporated into the final prices charged.

Principle 8

Only business can save the planet

> **Key takeaway:** The environmental crisis has reached the point where individual-driven change is insufficient. While for-profit firms were the main cause of the problem, they are also the main hope for a solution. Scale is vital and large firms must do much more if we are to build a sustainable economy.

When we internalize Principle 7, we understand the scale of the required change, with two implications. First, we cannot get there with higher levels of consumption – at least, not with our current economic model that equates progress with waste.[1] Something more radical is essential. At the end of his documentary, *An Inconvenient Truth*, Al Gore famously presented a call to action – for viewers to "be part of the solution." Having sketched a vision of global calamity, however, Gore then implores the audience to go home and "change a light bulb" or "plant a tree":

> That's when it got really depressing. The immense disproportion between the magnitude of the problem Gore had described and the puniness of what he was asking us to do about it was enough to sink your heart.[2]

Second, it is not about the actions of the individual, however worthy, but the actions of the for-profit firm. And, in particular, it is the actions of large corporations that will matter most. Scale is central to any meaningful solution. While much of the focus remains on reusing shopping bags and banning drinking straws, the planet is deteriorating before our eyes. In spite of all the attention to this issue and all the micro actions taken, greenhouse gas emissions continue to rise:[3]

> The problem we face is far greater than anything portrayed by the media. … recycling aluminum cans in the company cafeteria and ceremonial tree plantings are about as effective as bailing out the *Titanic* with teaspoons.[4]

Only for-profit firms are able to deliver the necessary reforms on the scale and at the speed at which they must occur to avert widespread ecological devastation.

Sustainability

In 1987, *The Brundtland Report* was published. The report, which was named after its lead author, Gro Harlem Brundtland (Norwegian Prime Minister and chair of the United Nation's World Commission on Environment and Development), was established to investigate the sustainability of our economic development. As well as concluding that our current system is unsustainable, the committee provided a definition of what a sustainable system would look like:

> Sustainable development is development that meets the needs of the present without compromising the ability of future generations to meet their own needs.[5]

The discussion fostered by the report essentially defined the field of sustainability as concerned primarily with resource use (in particular, the rapid rate of depletion and accompanying waste).[6] As such, most people today understand *sustainability* to represent issues related to the natural environment.[7] Importantly, however, the report was also prescient in framing the central role of business as both the cause of the problem and also the best hope for a solution:

> The Brundtland Report, which inspired the 1992 Earth Summit in Rio de Janeiro that resulted in the Climate Change Convention and in turn the Kyoto Protocol, acknowledged that many "of the development paths of the industrialized nations are clearly unsustainable." However, it held fast to its embrace of development toward industrialized nation living standards as part of the solution, not part of the problem. "If large parts of countries of the global South are to avert economic, social, and environmental catastrophes, it is essential that global economic growth be revitalized," the report stated.[8]

In the debate over whether we should pursue sustainability via material sacrifice (produce and consume less) or technological innovation (produce and consume more effectively), *The Brundtland Report*, with the supporting legitimacy of the UN, came down firmly in favor of progress. This presents a clear paradox between the damage to the environment done so far by the industrial revolution and subsequent economic development, and the future potential contributions firms can make to create a more sustainable economic system. The key is to move quickly:

The world has warmed more than one degree Celsius since the Industrial Revolution. The Paris climate agreement ... hoped to restrict warming to two degrees. The odds of succeeding, according to a recent study based on current emissions trends, are one in 20. ... Keeping the planet to two degrees of warming, let alone 1.5 degrees, would require transformative action. It will take more than good works and voluntary commitments; it will take a revolution.[9]

Given the scale of the problem, large-scale business is central to any potential solution. While greenhouse gas emissions from energy use are an important source of global emissions, for example, they form only 35% of the total, with industry (21%), forestry and agriculture (24%), transportation (14%), and buildings (6%) contributing the remainder.[10] There is much work to do, especially given the inherent flaws in our economic system built on waste and materialism.

Waste

Waste is a central component of the economic model that drives the global economy. For the majority of for-profit firms, the more you buy of their products, the better they perform and the faster the economy grows. In other words, excessive consumption and quick turnover are essential. Whether we *need* a product is less important than whether we *want* it. And, if we buy something, the quicker we throw it away and buy another one, the better for all concerned. Restraint and conservation are not encouraged. When you realize that Starbucks goes through 4 billion disposable cups a year at its 30,000 locations worldwide,[11] you understand that refusing a straw or bringing your own reusable cup (even if you get all of your friends to do the same) pales in comparison to the scale of the action required to make a difference.

An important assumption of this economic model is that the world's resources are unlimited. When a company extracts a raw material and converts it into something consumers want to buy, the price covers only the costs the firm incurred during the extraction and conversion. For the most part, there is no charge associated with the replenishment of the resource (e.g., the cost of losing forever the precious metals used in smartphones not recycled) or the pollution emitted during consumption (e.g., when driving a car). In short, our economy is based on waste – the more the firm uses and customers discard, the higher a country's GDP, and the *stronger* its economy. A question worth asking is "Are we sinking under the weight of our disposable society?"[12]

According to the OECD, the average person creates 3.3lb (1.5kg) of rubbish a day in France, 2.7lb in Canada and no more than 2.3lb in Japan. By the OECD's reckoning, the average American produces 4.5lb a day, and more recent accounting puts the figure at over 7lb a day, less than a quarter of which is recycled.[13]

Our consumer-oriented economic model dictates that we trade-in our fully functioning old smartphone and buy a new model whenever one comes out, without thinking through the consequences of that exchange. The problem is particularly acute in terms of the electronic waste (*e-waste*) that we generate in the process. As electronic consumer goods become obsolete and are discarded, the vast array of toxic metals they contain inflict significant costs onto society. And the problem is only growing as "the worldwide accumulation of e-waste has more than doubled in the last nine years. … [Shortly], the annual total is predicted to surpass 57 million tons":[14]

> Though often laced with lead, mercury or other toxic substances, laptops and phones also contain valuable elements like gold, silver and copper. Yet barely 20 percent of the world's e-waste is collected and [recycled]. … the raw materials contained in e-waste were worth roughly $61 billion in 2016. … the gold in the world's e-waste equaled more than a tenth of the gold mined globally that year. … Based on e-waste disposal rates, Americans alone throw out phones worth $60 million in gold and silver every year.[15]

There is a similar story with the amount of plastic that we use and discard every day. Plastic, which was invented in the early twentieth century and commercialized in the 1950s, has become one of our most versatile materials – "Some 322m tons of plastic were produced in 2015, and that number is expected to double by 2025."[16] It is particularly useful in single-use applications, which are convenient in households (e.g., bottled water) and critical in hospitals (e.g., syringes and packaging), where hygiene is life and death. In addition to being so useful, of course, plastic is highly durable, which unfortunately makes it difficult to dispose of. In fact, since the 1950s, while "8.3bn tonnes [of plastic] has been created. … just 9% has been recycled, 12% incinerated and 79% has accumulated in landfills or the wider environment."[17] At the rate we are going, by 2050, it is estimated there will be "12 billion metric tons of plastic waste … in landfills or the natural environment"[18] and "more plastic than fish by weight in the oceans."[19]

Together, e-waste and plastic are poster children for the ecological consequences of our consumption-based economic model, which treats all resources as infinite and fails to fully account for the externalities created during the production process. Yet waste reduction, when approached with a more enlightened attitude, can be a potential source of differentiation. Walmart, for example, whose ex-CEO (Lee Scott) committed the firm to the goal of "zero waste" in 2005,[20] presents an excellent case-study of what this can look like in practice. Ever since, Walmart has been committed to minimizing the waste packaging that is processed through its stores:

> Our packaging team, for example, worked with our packaging supplier to reduce excessive packaging on some of our private-label Kid Connection

toy products. By making the packaging just a little bit smaller on one private brand of toys, we will use 497 fewer containers and generate freight savings of more than $2.4 million per year. Additionally, we'll save more than 38-hundred trees and more than a thousand barrels of oil.[21]

When a large corporation such as Walmart alters its business practices, it has immediate ramifications for its tens of thousands of suppliers that have to adapt to the firm's new demands. And, given that Walmart has over 11,000 stores worldwide, in 27 countries, it only has to make a minor change to produce a dramatic effect.[22] The reason we have concentrated laundry detergent, for example, is because Walmart (which is responsible for "approximately 25 percent of the liquid laundry detergent sold in the United States") told its suppliers it wanted to reduce packaging waste and transportation costs. Every three years, the firm estimates its decision saves "more than 400 million gallons of water; more than 95 million pounds of plastic resin; and more than 125 million pounds of cardboard."[23] For Walmart, the connection between waste reduction and its overarching strategy is clear. Driving waste out of its supply chain creates savings, which the firm passes on to its customers in the form of lower prices. The extension of this philosophy to its support of the Sustainable Product Index,[24] ultimately, is designed to enhance consumer awareness by allowing like-for-like comparison across all products in its stores. Equally important for Walmart, however, it will provide more data about its supply chain that the firm can use to drive costs even lower.

Examples such as these exist in many industries. Unfortunately, there are many more examples of waste and inefficiency. We use and dispose of far more resources than we conserve or recycle. A direct driver of this waste is the materialism that motivates our desire to consume.

Materialism

A characteristic of the developed world is that, as a general rule, our possessions vastly exceed our needs on a day-to-day basis. Perhaps it is part of our genetic inheritance from our hunter-gatherer days but, for some reason, we seem incapable of living within our means.[25] It is not clear that we are more prosperous as a result. It is a pity that, given our obvious capability for ingenuity, we have created an economic system that impoverishes as much as it enables:

> A quote from the former Vogue editor Diana Vreeland comes to mind: "Give 'em what they never knew they wanted." Fast-fashion retailers like H&M, Topshop and Forever 21 are great at hawking what we never knew we wanted. Not only that, they offer it at steadily reduced prices. … Quality is no longer an issue, because you need clothes to last just "until the next trend comes along."[26]

It is equally distressing that we are willing to place our superficial concern for material objects above the wellbeing of other humans. In addition to wasted resources, there are social and human costs to the mass-production of cheap T-shirts. We may believe that it improves our lives to have someone else do our hard work for us ("Today, the United States makes only 2 percent of the clothing its consumers purchase, compared with roughly 50 percent in 1990"),[27] but there is nothing sustainable (in a holistic sense) in manufacturing clothes thousands of miles away, shipping them to the West, all for under $10. Ultimately, we are all worse off as a result:

> The wastefulness encouraged by buying cheap and chasing the trends is obvious, but the hidden costs are even more galling. ... "disposable clothing" is damaging the environment, the economy and even our souls. ... Have we somehow become disconnected from ourselves? If we don't stop to consider this, we may end up perpetually rushing out to buy more "stuff," never realizing what we truly need, genuinely want and cannot afford to waste.[28]

In terms of stakeholder responses to firm behavior (a willingness to reward those firms that best meet expectations), we are constrained by our desire to consume, our insistence on convenience, and our fixation on price. In short, while there are any number of studies that report consumers' willingness to buy green or socially responsible products, there are many others that suggest we are all quite capable of saying one thing, while doing another.[29] Most individuals, when asked, want to believe they are ethical and persuade the person asking them that this is the case. When it comes time to purchase, however, we seem either to be unwilling or unable to put our ethical aspirations into practice. It seems that our best intentions are easily distracted and there is a limit for firms that rely too heavily on the market segment of ethical consumers:

> On the surface, there has seemingly never been a better time to launch a sustainable offering. Consumers – particularly Millennials – increasingly say they want brands that embrace purpose and sustainability. ... Yet a frustrating paradox remains at the heart of green business: Few consumers who report positive attitudes toward eco-friendly products and services follow through with their wallets. In one recent survey 65% said they want to buy purpose-driven brands that advocate sustainability, yet only about 26% actually do so.[30]

Driving our materialism to new depths is the concept of *conspicuous virtue* – the idea that it is the perception of a good, rather than its functional value, that drives the consumption of that good. An example of this might be a consumer who drives a Prius, primarily because they want to convey to others their concern for the environment. This focus on perceptions can rise to the point where it overrides the actual benefit to the environment that driving a Prius offers.[31] This idea also has parallels with what economists call a *Veblen good* – "a product that is valued and desirable simply for being more expensive." The idea of a Veblen good was introduced by Thorstein Veblen in 1899 in a sociological paper titled "Theory of the Leisure Class," which introduced the idea of conspicuous consumption. This idea can be twisted to highlight the idea of *conspicuous virtue*:

> Conspicuous consumption stays with us today. But increasingly, it seems [that] many consumers are not seeking an outright demonstration of wealth. Instead, they consume to demonstrate their innate goodness. They spend not to suggest the deepness of their pockets but the deepness of their hearts. We inhabit, to update Veblen, an age of conspicuous virtue.[32]

Conspicuous virtue arises when consumers purchase "virtuous goods" largely in order to demonstrate their virtuousness, rather than for the instrumental value of the goods themselves. The goal is "to make a statement. It is not only to do right, whatever that might mean, but to announce that you are doing so."[33] Cynics suggest that this idea of conspicuous virtue helps explain the popularity of goods such as the *Livestrong* yellow wristband[34] that, simultaneously, raised money for cancer research, while allowing the donor (who only needed to donate a small amount) to demonstrate to the world that they support the cause:

> No doubt some wear the bands in solidarity, or for inspiration – but, that said, the wristband conceit was simply ingenious. It allowed people to make a show of their virtue. They could give to a good cause, and they could advertise their caring to everyone else.[35]

Related to this issue of conspicuousness is the idea that the visibility of something (rather than the actual harm being done) determines our reaction to it. This phenomenon, discussed in terms of consumption here, has an important application to the debate around sustainability and was most forcibly brought home during the Deepwater Horizon oil spill, the largest environmental disaster to have occurred in the U.S. and the largest ocean oil spill anywhere, ever.[36] While the Deepwater spill deservedly prompted public outrage, there is a much more serious and long-lasting form of pollution in the Gulf of Mexico that continues, but is routinely ignored. It is caused by the phosphate/nitrogen run-off from fertilizers used in farms along the Mississippi river. The excess runs off into the river and then flows down to the Gulf, causing a "dead zone" that is much bigger and damaging than the Deepwater Horizon oil spill. Because we cannot see it (and because of the strength of the farm lobby in Washington DC), however, it does not garner much media attention and even less public concern.[37] Similarly, while we get angry about rivers catching fire,[38] we cannot see the build-up of carbon dioxide (and many other pollutants) in the atmosphere, which helps explain why more people are not as outraged about the problem and motivated to act.

Scale

In order to quantify the scale of the challenge humanity faces in creating a more sustainable economic system, it is instructive to understand not only the extent of the damage done to date but, perhaps more importantly, the pace at which we continue to do harm:

> Everyone knows what must be done about climate change, but no one is doing anything about it. More than two decades of speeches and summitry have failed to thin out emissions of greenhouse gases. In fact, emissions are accelerating: a quarter of all the carbon dioxide pumped into the air by humans was put there in the decade between 2000 and 2010. It will hang around for centuries, meaning that the future is sure to be hotter, even if all greenhouse-gas emissions cease overnight. The official ambition of limiting the global temperature rise to 2°C looks increasingly like a bad joke.[39]

As a result of the enormity of the challenge, a large-scale response is required. *Large scale*, however, is not currently where we are at as a society:

> Like recycling, re-using carrier bags has become something of an iconic "sustainable behaviour." But whatever else its benefits may be, it is not, in itself, an especially good way of cutting carbon. Like all simple and painless behavioural changes, its value hangs on whether it acts as a catalyst for other, more impactful, activities or support for political changes.[40]

Although changes such as recycling aluminum cans, or using reusable shopping bags, or buying fairtrade coffee, or changing lightbulbs at home make us feel like we are taking action; in reality, we are not even scratching the surface of the problem. For the overall effect to be meaningful, the positive environmental actions need to outweigh the negative, need to do so worldwide, and need to touch all aspects of our lives. Unfortunately, we are far from achieving this. The danger, of course, is that, if we convince ourselves we are doing something, it provides us with the *moral license* to avoid making the difficult decisions necessary to generate meaningful reform. The solution, as with all the ideas discussed in this book, depends on stakeholders demanding change and then being willing to enforce that change:

> Clearly, economic systems do not overhaul themselves – and in a democracy, majority support is a prerequisite for any significant societal shift.

Politicians do not take risks if they don't think the electorate will support them. And civil society cannot function without a diverse supporter-base.[41]

The issues discussed in Principle 8 (and indirectly throughout the book) rely on the assumption that society today owes an obligation to future generations to leave them a planet that is functional. If we accept this broad, inter-generational obligation, the question then becomes: *How much should we be willing to pay today to minimize the future costs of our current actions?* Long ago, Howard Bowen was thinking about "the responsibilities of a business toward future generations as distinct from the present generation" and the difficult tradeoffs involved:

> How rapidly and in what manner should it utilize nonreplaceable natural resources? What provision should be made for replacement of timber, fish, and other reproducible natural resources? Is the destruction of arable land through strip mining ethically defensible? These are extremely diffi-cult questions because there are no clear principles to determine precisely how the interests of future generations should be balanced against those of present generations, or to what extent private business should be called upon to look out for future generations.[42]

This issue is particularly relevant in terms of issues such as climate change, but relates also to the broader issue of how to value future benefit against present-day cost. One attempt to do that was the influential Stern report on climate change,[43] which argued that society must "value the welfare of all present and future citizens equally and give no special preference to current voters."[44] The difficulty is, of course, how to account for the possibility of unknowns such as technical innovation and the greater wealth of future generations and, as a result, avoid exaggerating the immediate cost implications of climate change (and causing unnecessary present–day suffering). Getting this balance between current and future obligations *correct* is crucial if we are to ensure an effective and realizable response to this hugely important issue:

> The problem of weighting the present and the future equally is that there is a lot of future. The number of future generations is potentially so large that small but permanent benefit to them would justify great sacrifice now. If we were to use this criterion to appraise all long-term invest-ment, the volume of such investment would impoverish the current population. ... The burden of caring for all humanity, present and future, is greater than even the best-intentioned of us can bear.[45]

While it appears that our capacity for altruism toward future generations is limited, perhaps we can act to save ourselves. The speed at which climate change is occurring suggests we will see dramatic consequences in our lifetime. If so, sustainability increasingly represents a present-day imperative. Although all the warnings may motivate us to act, however, human nature suggests that meaningful change will most likely occur only in the face of impending doom. At that time, it will require more dramatic change in a shorter timeframe at a much higher cost (if it is possible at all). Given the radical changes in behavior that will be required of people in both developed and developing countries, even if we start seriously today, it is therefore preferable that buy-in is secured as quickly as possible and large corporations are recruited to help us respond:

> Here's a question. Which trio of companies has done more for the environment … Patagonia, Starbucks and Chipotle? Or Walmart, Coca-Cola and McDonald's? … Patagonia, Starbucks and Chipotle have been path-breaking companies when it comes to sustainability, but Walmart, Coca-Cola and McDonald's are so much bigger that, despite their glaring flaws, and the fundamental problems with their business models, they will have a greater impact as they get serious about curbing their environmental footprint, and that of their suppliers.[46]

While provocative, the answer to the question is intuitive. That is not to say that the question isn't an important one to ask. Perhaps, for the CSR/sustainability community, it is the only one worth asking. Ultimately, the core question is: Are we interested in *ideal possibilities* or *meaningful change*? If *change* is what we want, then Walmart, Coca-Cola, and McDonald's need to be the source. That is not to diminish the wonderful business models of other smaller companies, especially Patagonia and Starbucks. If anything, they are the roadmap for what larger firms also need to accomplish. But, unless the largest firms are fully invested in *Sustainable Value Creation* (*SVC*), we will only be working at the periphery of the progress that needs to be made.

This conundrum plays out at a micro level whenever we make the effort to recycle a plastic bottle or aluminum can – it is still the environmentally responsible thing to do, even though we know the effect on the planet's future is limited, especially in light of the huge amount of resources that are wasted elsewhere in our economic system every day. It is not even clear that the item will be recycled[47] and, if it is, it is not clear that recycling results in less environmental impact. Just as building more roads encourages more people to drive and we know that "recycling programs do increase recycling rates, studies have shown that they also increase total consumption."[48]

For-profit firms are the most valuable organizational form because it is only these organizations that can act with the efficiency required on the scale necessary to implement meaningful reform in the timeframe within which change is needed. Yet, in order for this to occur, we need to ask firms to take on this task. The for-profit firm is simply a tool we have devised to solve a specific problem – how to allocate scarce and valuable resources to achieve optimal outcomes (a problem that has challenged humanity throughout our existence). The best solution we have found to date is for-profit firms operating within a market-based, democratic form of capitalism. Once you understand firms are merely a tool, however, you understand that they will do what we ask of them. If we ask them to pollute the planet (as we are, at present), they will do that, very efficiently. Equally, if we ask them to preserve the planet, they will find the most efficient means of achieving that goal. They will do what we want them to do – they reflect our collective set of values. Yet, within the vast group of organizations labeled *for-profit firms*, there are clearly some that contain vastly more potential for significant impact. Massive firms have a disproportionate impact on our daily lives. The market capitalization of the Top 10 global firms alone is $6.5 trillion.[49] What these large firms do in the near future, therefore, will do more to influence our lifestyles, standard of living, and future security than all of the smaller firms combined. As Jason Clay states in his TED talk on how big brands can save biodiversity:

> 100 companies control 25% of the trade of all 15 of the most significant commodities on the planet. … Why is 25% important? Because if these companies demand sustainable products they will pull 40–50% of production.[50]

According to Clay, it is all about the B2B supply chain. Suppliers are as important a stakeholder to the firm as the customer. Large companies pushing other large companies will achieve change much faster and on a scale that actually matters than waiting for consumers, one-by-one, to wake up to the global consequences of their consumption decisions.

Summary

Principle 8 states that *Only business can save the planet*. The core argument rests on the idea that, in order to solve the climate crisis, scale and speed are essential – that the problem has reached a point where only radical and rapid change will produce meaningful effects and help avert the catastrophic outcome we are hurtling toward. In this light, while for-profit firms are the main cause of the environmental mess we face, they are also the main hope for a solution, as long as we ask them to tackle the task. There is much work to do, both in terms of production and consumption, in order to create a truly *sustainable* economic system.

Principle 9

Value creation is not a choice

> **Key takeaway:** *SVC* is a philosophy of management that infuses the firm, incorporating all aspects of business. Value creation is, therefore, not something firms can choose to do. By definition, they are already doing it, at least to some degree; it is just that some do it better than others.

As indicated in Principle 8, fundamental change on a massive scale (and quickly) is necessary if we are to build a more sustainable economic system. *Sustainable Value Creation (SVC)* provides an actionable solution to this problem, but only if the radical nature of this managing philosophy is properly understood. Value creation is not a peripheral activity; it is central to everything the firm does. As such, it is not something firms can choose to do. All firms already create value for at least some of their stakeholders, some of the time. The goal is for more firms to do it for more of their stakeholders, more of the time.

Not philanthropy, but core operations

SVC, unlike contemporary CSR, is not about philanthropy,[1] but day-to-day operations. If any money is being spent by the firm on areas not directly related to core competencies, it is likely not the most efficient use of that money. If, however, the main justification for an expenditure is brand awareness and the firm feels there is value in being associated with a particular charity or good cause (in other words, if the values underpinning the cause align with those of the firm's stakeholders), then that investment should be made, but responsibility for it should be placed where it belongs, in the marketing department. That functional area contains experts who know best how to manage the brand. If, however, there are other business–related reasons for the firm to donate money to a specific cause, such as to motivate employees, then responsibility for that decision should lie with the relevant functional area – it should be part of the firm's core functions so that the relevant expertise can be applied for optimal, value-added effect:

Consider Subaru of America. In the first nine months of this year, 512 employees have volunteered their time for 105 events for 46 different organizations. Seventy-four employees donated 500 hours to build three Habitat for Humanity homes in Camden, N.J., a poor city a few minutes from Subaru's headquarters in Cherry Hill. On the West Coast, 88 employees have donated 270 hours to assemble wheelchairs that were donated to veterans. Employees have filled 2,000 backpacks for school-children. For a company like Subaru, with a brand image of being out-doors, dependable, inclusive and kind, those metrics help attract great employees. They also help the company's marketing campaign.[2]

The connection between value creation and philanthropy is tangential, at best. Although there are specific tax advantages associated with donations, the main business-related reason for making the payment is the potential market-ing benefits, if employed strategically. Unless there is a direct connection to operations, the argument for firms donating large sums in areas in which they have low levels of expertise is difficult to make. One reason for this is that, not only is philanthropy likely inefficient if it is unrelated to core operations, but it can also go largely unrewarded (or even unrecognized) by the stake-holders it is sometimes designed to placate:

Walmart is extremely generous, giving away over $1bn in cash and product annually – but it's still viewed by the public as one of the least responsible companies on the planet, and is a continual target of boycotts and protests.[3]

What if corporate America was willing to take the more than $18bn it donates annually[4] and, instead, invest it in what it does best – operating its business? For-profit firms should focus on identifying those problems for which there is a clear market-based solution and then deliver that solution in an efficient and socially responsible manner. The idea of *SVC* as a managing philosophy focuses on firms' areas of expertise throughout all aspects of oper-ations and de-emphasizes actions that stray outside that expertise for which there either is not a market solution, or the firm is not well-equipped to deliver that solution. That is how value is optimized over the medium to long term – by operating in a way that seeks to meet the needs and demands of the firm's stakeholders, broadly defined. In other words, the focus of busi-ness remains the same; it is the way the organization goes about it that is different with an *SVC* perspective.

Not caring capitalism, but market capitalism

In recent years, there have been growing calls to reinvent capitalism – with some going as far as to advocate for the introduction of socialism.[5] High-profile actors, such as Bill Gates of Microsoft ("caring capitalism") and

Muhammad Yunus of Grameen Bank ("social business"), have sought to reform the underlying principles of capitalist ideology by urging firms to adopt goals beyond a focus on profit. More recently, work has begun to develop the concept of "inclusive capitalism, which is the idea that those with the power and the means have a responsibility to help make society stronger and more inclusive for those who don't."[6]

As discussed throughout this book, *SVC* rejects these attempts as not only futile, but counter-productive. It is not the *ends* of capitalism (profit) that matter so much as the *means* by which the ends are pursued.[7] Although efforts to deter firms from the pursuit of profit are delivered with the best of intentions, the difficulty in implementation quickly becomes apparent when these ideas are investigated in greater detail. Bill Gates, for example, launched his manifesto for a "new system" of capitalism in a speech at the World Economic Forum at Davos in 2008:

> I like to call this new system creative capitalism – an approach where governments, businesses, and nonprofits work together to stretch the reach of market forces so that more people can make a profit, or gain recognition, doing work that eases the world's inequities.[8]

While appealing at first glance, it is not clear what Gates actually means by "creative capitalism" and how it is to be realized in practice. For example, it is easy to say that:

> I hope corporations will consider dedicating a percentage of your top innovators' time to issues that could help people left out of the global economy. ... It is a great form of creative capitalism, because it takes the brainpower that makes life better for the richest, and dedicates it to improving the lives of everyone else.[9]

But, in reality, how is a firm to decide which issue it should prioritize and devote its most valuable resources? How much value is compromised because these "top innovators" are working on a philanthropic problem (that may or may not be suited to their particular skillset) instead of one based on market demand? How are firms to determine exactly which projects are *appropriate* and which are not? Do firms need to calculate a certain level of potential social welfare in advance? If so, how would they do that? What if it is not realized? None of these questions are addressed sufficiently, with Gates weaving back-and-forth between an argument based on market forces and one based on an appeal to firms' altruism without any clear guidance as to how priorities among competing claims should be set. As one supportive commentator noted:

> In Gates' vision, private companies should be encouraged to tweak their structure slightly to free up their innovative thinkers to work on solutions

to problems in the developing world. It's gung-ho, rather than hairshirt, philanthropy. ... While companies or individuals may ultimately profit from this work in developing nations, the reward primarily comes in the form of recognition and enjoyment.[10]

On an individual/micro level, such arguments are appealing, romantic even; but, at a macro level, they quickly fall apart. In contrast, this book argues that the market, while imperfect, remains the best means society has for allocating scarce resources. As noted by a critic of caring capitalism:

> there is a stronger argument to be made against "creative capitalism," and it is that profits come from serving society. The larger the profits, the better job the company tends to have done. Profit maximization is a worthy goal by itself.[11]

Put more bluntly, *SVC*, implemented throughout the firm via a stakeholder perspective and a focus on medium- to long-term value creation, optimizes performance:

> Sure, let those who have become rich under capitalism try to do good things for those who are still poor, as Mr. Gates has admirably chosen to do. But a New-Age blend of market incentives and feel-good recognition will not end poverty. History has shown that profit-motivated capitalism is still the best hope for the poor.[12]

Similar criticisms can be leveled against Muhammad Yunus, the 2006 winner of the Nobel Peace Prize, whose concept of "social business" touches on ideas similar to those expressed by Gates.[13] In reality, what both men are expressing is a form of social entrepreneurship, which demands that firms replace profit-seeking with something that amounts to altruism:

> "Social business" marks a transition from the imaginative to the quixotic, envisaging a new sector of the economy made up of companies run as private businesses but making no profits. These would focus on products and services that conventional companies do not find profitable, such as healthcare, nutrition, housing and sanitation for the poor. It is predicated on the view that investors will be happy to get zero return as long as they can see returns in social benefits.[14]

Such business models have limited market appeal – while some consumers are willing to pay the associated price premiums, the evidence suggests that such charitable motivations cannot be assumed market-wide. In advocating such a philosophy, Yunus is turning his back on the sound business model for which he won his Nobel Prize. Microfinance (and Grameen Bank, the organization founded by Yunus to deliver microloans to individuals who cannot secure them from mainstream financial institutions) was effective because it extended the market to consumers whose demand was thought to be insufficient for traditional finance models. All it took was a product tailored to the specific needs of a specific segment of the market. While microfinance is an industry that is grounded in business fundamentals, however, it is not clear how Yunus expects altruism to constitute sufficient incentive to mobilize the private sector as a whole:

> The genius of microfinance was in getting the profit motive to work for the very poorest. The drawback of social business is that it depends on the kindness of strangers.[15]

Not sharing value, but creating value

The ideas of "caring capitalism" and "social business" present leaps of faith and logic that are similar to those generated by the idea of "shared value." Similar to Gates and Yunus, Michael Porter and Mark Kramer have enjoyed a significant amount of publicity for their idea, which also attempts to over-turn centuries of economic theory and practice to reinvent the firm:

> The purpose of the corporation must be redefined as creating shared value, not just profit per se.[16]

On the surface, Porter's shared value (or caring capitalism) and *SVC* can appear to produce similar behavior. The motivating force is different, however, and this is important because it will lead to different outcomes in terms of the venture's ultimate success or failure. The difference comes down to the focus of the firm and the relevance to core operations of the issue at hand. Starbucks, for example, should not form partnerships with shade-grown coffee farmers in Guatemala because it recognizes those farmers face an uncertain future with an insufficient welfare net to support them if their businesses fail (a non-operational goal), but because Starbucks needs to secure a stable supply of high-quality coffee beans and supporting these farmers in a sustainable manner is the best way to guarantee that supply (an operational goal). In other words, Starbucks should form stable and lasting partnerships with these key suppliers not because it is seeking to fill a charitable social need; the firm should do it because these farmers produce a raw material that is essential to its business. Starbucks is incentivized to protect the raw material in a sustainable way, rather than ruthlessly exploit it. If those Guatemalan farmers are not producing a product that is in demand (i.e., if the business logic for a relationship is not there), the argument that Starbucks should get involved is difficult to make.

Ultimately, although for-profit firms can help with the first perspective (caring capitalism), they are much better suited to the second perspective (market capitalism). Ideally, it is the role of governmental and nonprofit sectors to focus on those problems that the market ignores or cannot solve. In contrast, Porter and Kramer argue that charitable goals should be considered equally with operational goals and firms should then utilize their market-based skills and expertise to solve both kinds of problem – in other words, that they should become less like for-profit firms and more like nonprofit organizations or government agencies. But, the challenges with this notion again quickly become apparent when a firm tries to implement these ideas in practice. To turn back to the Starbucks example, above – because Starbucks is forming ties with Guatemalan coffee growers due to their value to the firm's core business, the way they structure their proposed solution is different than if they were forming the ties for other, more altruistic reasons. As it is, Starbucks provides the farmers with financial security (by providing long-term contracts and guaranteeing an above-market price for their beans) but, in return, secures guarantees of quality and the right (and incentive) to be directly involved in training the farmers to ensure the coffee is prepared in exactly the way the firm needs it to be. In other words, the motivation for the engagement is central to the value of the solution provided. Encouraging firms to adopt altruistic motivations is not an effective plan for "how to fix capitalism" but, instead, represents a misunderstanding of what profit is and how it is generated. As suggested by other critics of these attempts to reinvent capitalism:[17]

> Rosabeth Moss Kanter warned of the pitfalls for companies that make "social commitments that do not have an economic logic that sustains the enterprise by attracting resources." More companies are learning to reap commercial benefits from strategies that have a wider social value. That's great. But the basic job of coaxing capitalism in the right direction is the same as it always has been: find ways to harness society's needs to companies' self-interest and hope the two stay together.[18]

It is naive to suggest that companies should exist primarily to solve problems motivated by altruism. Business is the solution to market problems/opportunities that create value as a direct consequence. Firms optimize value, broadly defined, by combining scarce and valuable resources to meet market needs, while considering the interests of a broad range of stakeholders and seeking to provide sustainable shareholder returns over the medium to long term. Firms can often use their expertise to assist in meeting non-operational goals, but this should not be their primary concern. Instead, governments and nonprofits exist to meet social needs where gaps in the market occur.

The difference between a firm with *SVC* integrated fully throughout the organization (encompassing strategic decision-making and all aspects of day-to-day operations) and a firm that ignores the ideas discussed in this book is not whether its CEO donates to charity, but is reflected in the way the firm operates the core aspects of its business. There is a better way to create more value for the firm's suppliers, to pay your employees, to comply with laws, for example, and there is a worse way to create less value for these key constituents. Those firms that seek to implement *SVC* through core operations will add more value than any amount of philanthropy can achieve.

The consequence of internalizing the discussion above is the realization that *Value creation is not a choice*. It is not a choice because *SVC* is not about philanthropy and is more than brand insurance;[19] it is not about "caring capitalism" and is not about "sharing value." *SVC* is about the firm's core operations – creating value for stakeholders, broadly defined, by focusing on the firm's areas of expertise to solve market-based problems. Because the scale and scope of *SVC* is so thoroughly embedded in core operations, it is not something the firm can choose to do; it is the way business is conducted. When a firm hires an employee, engages with a supplier, responds to a regulator, sells a product, or does any one of the many hundreds of things it does every day, it is creating value. All of these business decisions have economic, social, moral, and ethical dimensions, and they touch on all of the firm's stakeholders at least some of the time. As such, *SVC* is not something that can be ignored or relegated in importance – it is what firms do; it is just that some firms do it better and more deliberately than others. Vigilant and informed stakeholders who engage with firms to promote their values will ensure that this measure of performance will increasingly become a predictor of market success.

Once firms understand that they are embedded in complex stakeholder relations and that they need to manage these relations effectively if they are to survive and thrive over the medium to long term in today's global business environment, then strategic planning and daily operations represent the means to manage the messy tradeoffs and priority-setting. Certainly, firms are either better or worse at managing these relationships and they draw the lines of key stakeholders narrowly (at shareholders alone) or more broadly (in terms of a wider group of constituents). Either way, creating value is not an option, it is *the* way that business is conducted. Understanding and applying the underlying principles detailed in this book will help firms be more effective at creating value and building an organization that is both competitive and sustainable.

Summary

Principle 9 states that *Value creation is not a choice*. *SVC* is a management philosophy that is intricately woven into every decision the firm makes. It is not about peripheral activities, such as philanthropy, but about how the firm treats its employees and suppliers and customers, and all of its stakeholders. It is not about being compassionate or sharing value; it is about a firm doing what it does best – applying its technical expertise to build a competitive advantage to solve a market-based problem (from which society benefits). As such, *SVC* is not a choice; it is integral to all aspects of operations. There is simply no choice to be made. All firms create value (like all firms do strategy, marketing, and so on) – it is just that some do it better than others.

Principle 10

The *business* of business is business

Key takeaway: Milton Friedman believed that firms should prioritize economic success. Similarly, *SVC* is all about strategy, day-to-day decisions, and core operations. The pursuit of profit and value creation are synonymous. Business serves society best when it focuses primarily on business.

As presented in Principle 9, *Sustainable Value Creation* (*SVC*) is not about issues that are peripheral to the firm and is not about reinventing capitalism. Rather, it is about improving day-to-day decisions supporting strategy and core operations to create value for stakeholders, broadly defined. As a result, I believe that *SVC*, as a management philosophy, is fully compatible with Milton Friedman's belief that business serves society best when it focuses primarily on *business*.

Milton Friedman

Milton Friedman was right – the social responsibility of business is *business*. In Friedman's own words, what he meant by this is that:

> In a free-enterprise, private-property system, a corporate executive is an employee of the owners of the business. He has direct responsibility to his employers. That responsibility is to conduct the business in accordance with their desires, which generally will be to make as much money as possible *while conforming to the basic rules of the society, both those embodied in law and those embodied in ethical custom.* (emphasis added)[1]

Friedman argued, essentially, that conducting business in a way that produces the best possible outcomes for the firm's shareholders, over the long run, involves playing by the rules of the game. And, although he did not say it directly, it is implicit in his argument that it is the firm's stakeholders, collectively, who determine those rules. *SVC* supports this economic view.

Stakeholders have always shaped the rules by which society operates, consciously or otherwise, and they will continue to do so. The questions that are essential for any manager to ask, therefore, is *What are the rules today?* and *What are they likely to be tomorrow?* The rules are always changing, but the aggregate effect of millions of people making millions of decisions everyday determines the overall context in which firms must act. Corporations cannot force consumers to buy their products, as long as consumers are willing to make their purchase decisions based on something other than convenience or the lowest price. Similarly, corporations cannot prevent the enactment of legislation, as long as politicians are willing to prioritize governing over campaign contributions and lobbying pressures. And corporations cannot force employees to work for abusive pay levels, as long as workers ensure they have the skillset to demand higher pay and better conditions. Each of these decisions is a value judgment made by one of the firm's stakeholders. Managers, therefore, need to understand the values that underpin these decisions at any given point in time because they have operational consequences for the firm. Those managers that understand the rules most completely are best placed to help their firm succeed by aligning the firm's actions with the underlying values of its stakeholders.

While the business of business is *business*, the goal of this book has been to build the argument that how this business is conducted matters. The concept of *SVC*, therefore, constitutes a roadmap for the manager seeking to conduct business successfully in the twenty-first century because, rather than obsess about what the firm does (generate profits), *SVC* is more focused on how the firm does it. In other words, framing the argument is key, and policies or practices that lower costs and/or raise revenues over the medium to long term are of primary importance. In order to illustrate this, let's return to the debate between a living wage and a minimum wage: Does a firm pay its employees a living wage because it feels that they deserve something better; or does it pay them a living wage because it understands that the investment raises morale and loyalty, increases productivity, and decreases the recruitment and training costs that are associated with higher turnover? As Paul Polman, the ex-CEO of Unilever puts it:

> To pay a textile worker in Pakistan 11 cents an hour doesn't make good business sense. … [Before I became CEO] We had a lot of contingent labour or we outsourced it and we looked at that as a cost item but we had a tremendous amount of turnover. Now we pay more and we have greater loyalty, more energy and higher productivity.[2]

Similarly, as discussed in Principle 9: Does Starbucks pay its suppliers of high-quality, shade-grown Arabica beans an above-market price because it feels morally or ethically responsible for farmers who do not earn sufficient wages in a country with an inadequate welfare safety-net, or does it pay those *fair trade* prices because it needs to secure a guaranteed supply of its most essential raw material? Whatever you think about Starbucks' coffee, Starbucks thinks it makes great coffee. As such, the firm risks its core business (whether you see

Starbucks as a café or as a "third place" between home and work) if it loses access to high-quality beans. It is therefore in the firm's best strategic interest to ensure the producers of its most highly prized raw material are incentivized to remain in business and continue to supply the firm over the long term. These ideas and the underlying philosophy that drives them are wholly consistent with Friedman's work.

The purpose of the firm

Although Milton Friedman wrote many books and articles in his career, perhaps the one for which he is best known (and most widely cited) within the CSR community is the article he published in *The New York Times* in 1970, "The Social Responsibility of Business is to Increase its Profits."[3] In the article, in which the economist is at his inflammatory best, Friedman argues that profit, as a result of the firm's actions, is an end in itself. He believes strongly that a firm need not have any additional justification for existing and that, in fact, social value is optimized when firms focus solely on pursuing their self-interest by attempting to generate profit:

> I share Adam Smith's skepticism about the benefits that can be expected from "those who affected to trade for the public good." … in a free society, … "there is one and only one social responsibility of business – to use its resources and engage in activities designed to increase its profits."[4]

Friedman's article is often contrasted against a 2002 article in *Harvard Business Review*, titled "What's a Business For?" by the influential British management commentator, Charles Handy.[5] In contrast to Friedman, Handy presents a much broader view of the purpose of business in society. For Handy, it is not sufficient to justify a firm's profit as an end in itself. For Handy, a business has to have a motivation other than merely making money to justify its existence – profit is merely a means to achieve a larger end. A firm should not remain in existence just because it is profitable, but because it is meeting a need that society *as a whole* values:

> It is salutary to ask about any organization, "If it did not exist, would we invent it? Only if it could do something better or more useful than anyone else" would have to be the answer, and profit would be the means to that larger end.[6]

On the surface, the positions taken by Friedman and Handy appear irreconcilable, and that is how they are often treated by the CSR community. Indeed, Friedman seems to go out of his way to antagonize CSR advocates by arguing that socially responsible behavior is a waste of the firm's resources, which legally (in his view, cf. Principle 2) belong to the firm's shareholders and not the firm's managers:

That is why, in my book *Capitalism and Freedom*, I have called [social responsibility] a "fundamentally subversive doctrine" in a free society.[7]

But, on closer analysis, their arguments are not nearly as far apart as they initially appear. Incorporating the ideas underpinning *SVC* narrows the gap between the two positions considerably. First, it is necessary to ask: If the purpose of the firm is to meet a need that society values as a whole (as Handy argues), what is the best means we have of quantifying that value? As discussed in Principle 6, *profit* is by far the most accurate method we have of capturing total value – not perfect, but it is difficult to imagine a more complete (or more elegant) measure. If true, then surely the most profitable firms are adding the most value (as Friedman argues). Again, the correlation is imperfect but, as a general rule, the relationship between profit and value holds.

Second, for additional consideration that Friedman and Handy are not as far apart as many believe, consider the following two questions:

- Does it make sense for a large financial firm to donate money to a group researching the effects of climate change because the CEO believes this is an important issue?
- Does it make sense for an oil firm to donate money to the same group because it perceives climate change to be a threat to its business model and wants to mitigate that threat by investigating possible alternatives?

The action, a large for-profit firm donating money to a nonprofit group, is the same. The difference is the relevance of the nonprofit's activities to the firm's core operations. Most level-headed CSR advocates would at least question the first action as a potential waste of money (incorporating Friedman's argument that the actions represent an inefficient, and potentially fraudulent, allocation of resources in an area in which the firm has no expertise), while the second action is a strategic question for a firm that needs to address issues that are important to key stakeholder groups in its operating environment.

Taking the arguments of Friedman and Handy in their entirety, therefore, a more insightful interpretation suggests that, to the extent that it is in a firm's interests to meet the needs of its key stakeholders (who determine their own positions and actions based on a complicated mix of ethics, values, and self-interest), the firm should do so. And, perhaps more importantly, by doing so, the firm can deliver the greatest value to the widest range of its stakeholders. From Handy's perspective, this point is easy to argue, but Friedman also recognizes this. He qualifies his statement that a manager's primary responsibility is to the shareholders of the enterprise, who seek "to make as much money as possible," for example, by noting that this pursuit must be tempered "while conforming to the basic rules of the society, *both those embodied in law and those embodied in ethical custom.*" In addition, a firm's actions are acceptable, only as long as it "engages in open and free competition *without deception or fraud*"[8] (emphasis added).

In qualifying his statements in this way (leaving a loophole in his argument big enough to drive any ethical or moral bus through), Friedman clearly outlines a duty for business to conform to society's expectations. And, in contrast to the inflammatory rhetoric he often used to convey his points, he is allowing for those societal expectations that are expressed both formally, in law, and informally, in norms and everyday conventions. Most people normally read the first half of Friedman's sentences and get annoyed but, in the examples provided above, it is the second half that provides the context in which the total sentence should be interpreted. Given that the ends of the organization that Handy portrays are to reinforce the values of the societies in which it operates, the similarities between the two men become even more apparent. This overlap was also noted by Archie Carroll, one of the most important thinkers on CSR, in his pivotal 1991 *Business Horizons* article that details his idea of the four corporate responsibilities in the Pyramid of CSR:

> Economist Milton Friedman ... has argued that social matters are not the concern of business people and that these problems should be resolved by the unfettered workings of the free market system. Friedman's argument loses some of its punch, however, when you consider his assertion in its totality. ... Most people focus on the first part of Friedman's quote but not the second part. It seems clear from this statement that profits, conformity to the law, and ethical custom embrace three components of the CSR pyramid – economic, legal, and ethical. That only leaves the philanthropic component for Friedman to reject. Although it may be appropriate for an economist to take this view, one would not encounter many business executives today who exclude philanthropic programs from their firms' range of activities.[9]

Rather than the result of this softening being presented as a reason for Friedman's argument to lose "some of its punch," however, I would argue that it reinforces the importance of incorporating Friedman's ideas within the intellectual framework underpinning *SVC*. As long as an argument can be made that any particular decision is in the best business interests of the firm, then I believe that is something that Milton Freidman would agree lies within the definition of *business*. In other words, while this book does not represent any kind of endorsement of Friedman's complete economic perspective (at a bare minimum, he mischaracterized the legal relationship between a firm and its shareholders), it does argue that *SVC* is compatible with the economic rationale that all of a firm's actions should reinforce its economic interests. As such, *SVC*, built on a foundation of iterative, long-term ties to all of the firm's stakeholders, offers managers a roadmap to survive and thrive in today's complex, dynamic business environment.

To be sure, the philosophy of *SVC* is demanding. It requires engagement – the idea that stakeholders must act in order to shape society in their collective interests. It also requires firms to respond to these demands and, where possible, to anticipate them. But, again, as long as stakeholders are willing to enforce their values and beliefs, conforming to those expectations is in the firm's economic interest. *SVC* is not a passive philosophy; it is proactive, but the result is a society that is *shaped*, rather than one that *forms*. If stakeholders are motivated to change the rules in a way that promotes value, broadly defined, then for-profit firms are the best means we have of interpreting those new standards and responding more rapidly and efficiently than any other organizational form in any other economic system.

Summary

Principle 10 states that *The* business *of business is business*. It argues that *SVC* is not about issues peripheral to the firm, but instead focuses on day-to-day decisions, strategic planning, and core operations. Equally important, it does so in a way that accounts for the complex, dynamic business environment in which firms must operate. As such, *SVC* is a philosophy of management designed to generate business success. And, because this success (i.e., profit) optimizes value when the firm meets the needs and demands of its broad range of stakeholders, it is compatible with Milton Friedman's arguments that firms benefit society the most when they focus on business.

Conclusion
Sustainable Value Creation

The ideas detailed in this book revolve around the ten principles that define *Sustainable Value Creation (SVC)*. That is, in a dynamic environment defined by the actions and decisions of a firm's broad set of stakeholders, value is optimized when the firm's stakeholders are willing to convey and enforce their needs, while the firm is willing to respond and, where possible, anticipate those changing needs. Thus, these economic and social exchanges, at their most fundamental, are interactions formed around the collective set of values prevalent in society at any given point and are best measured by the profit the firm is able to generate.

The Ten Defining Principles of *Sustainable Value Creation*

Principle 1 Business is social progress: There is a direct correlation between the amount of business in a society and the extent of progress enjoyed by that society. For-profit firms are the most effective means of achieving that progress.

Principle 2 Shareholders do not own the firm: Contrary to popular myth, shareholders are not the legal owners of the firm. Similarly, managers do not have a fiduciary responsibility to maximize shareholder value. Instead, the firm is an independent legal entity that should be run in the interests of its broad set of stakeholders.

Principle 3 Prioritizing competing stakeholder interests is difficult: Implementing *SVC* requires the firm to operate in the interests of its stakeholders, broadly defined. While identifying these stakeholders is easy, however, stakeholder theory will only be of practical value when it helps managers prioritize among competing stakeholder interests.

Principle 4 CSR is a stakeholder responsibility: CSR will only work if firms are rewarded for acting and punished for failing to act. As such, while CSR includes a *responsibility* for a firm to meet the needs and demands of its stakeholders, the stakeholders themselves have an equal, if not more important, *responsibility* to hold the firm to account.

Principle 5 Market-based solutions are optimal: In general, market forces generate superior outcomes than alternative means of allocating scarce and valuable resources, such as government mandate. While stakeholders have an interest in shaping the behavior of firms, the mechanism by which this occurs most effectively is the market.

Principle 6 Profit = total value: In essence, a firm's profit represents the ability to sell a good or service at a higher price than what it costs to produce. Production and consumption, however, are more than merely technical decisions. They encapsulate the total value (to all stakeholders) that is added by the firm.

Principle 7 The *free* market is not free: The free market is an illusion. It encourages firms to externalize costs that are borne by society rather than consumers; it is rife with subsidies and quotas that favor some firms and industries over others. The result is an economic system that is distorted and, as a result, unsustainable.

Principle 8 Only business can save the planet: The environmental crisis has reached the point where individual-driven change is insufficient. While for-profit firms were the main cause of the problem, they are also the main hope for a solution. Scale is vital and large firms must do much more if we are to build a sustainable economy.

Principle 9 Value creation is not a choice: *SVC* is a philosophy of management that infuses the firm, incorporating all aspects of business. Value creation is, therefore, not something firms can choose to do. By definition, they are already doing it, at least to some degree; it is just that some do it better than others.

Principle 10 The *business* of business is business: Milton Friedman believed that firms should prioritize economic success. Similarly, *SVC* is all about strategy, day-to-day decisions, and core operations. The pursuit of profit and value creation are synonymous. Business serves society best when it focuses primarily on business.

In conclusion, therefore, given the discussion of ideas and concepts in this book, how can we combine these ten core principles into a succinct definition of *SVC*?

Defining SVC

The goal of this book has been to frame *SVC* (CSR, redefined) in terms of a set of principles that differentiate it from existing definitions of CSR, and from related concepts such as sustainability and business ethics. While sustainability relates to issues of ecological preservation and business ethics seeks to construct normative prescriptions of *right* and *wrong*, *SVC* is a pragmatic philosophy grounded in the strategic planning and day-to-day operations of the firm. As such, *SVC* is central to the firm's value creating activities and, ultimately, its business success.

In constructing a working definition of *SVC* that draws upon the ten underlying principles, five components are essential: First, that a firm incorporates a CSR perspective within its culture and strategic planning process; second, that any actions it takes are directly related to core operations; third, that it seeks to understand and respond to the needs of all of its stakeholders; fourth, that it aims to optimize value created; and fifth, that it shifts from a short-term perspective to managing its resources and relations with key stakeholders over the medium to long term.[1]

Sustainable Value Creation

The incorporation of a holistic *CSR perspective* within a firm's strategic planning and *core operations* so that the firm is managed in the interests of a broad set of *stakeholders* to *optimize value* over the *medium to long term*.

Essential to any definition of *SVC* is the idea that a firm should incorporate a CSR perspective, as redefined in this framework, within its culture and strategic planning process. This CSR perspective presupposes an iterative relationship between the firm and all of its stakeholders, with equal responsibilities to convey needs and respond to those needs whenever possible (Principle 4). An important tool that helps the firm do this is a *stakeholder filter* integrated into the firm's operational decision-making processes. This filter is defined as a conceptual screen through which strategic and tactical decisions are evaluated for their impact on the firm's various stakeholders.[2] Embedding the profit incentive within a framework of guiding values further enables managers to implement *SVC* throughout all aspects of operations (Principle 10).

The second component of *SVC* is that any action a firm takes should be directly related to core operations. In short, the same action will differ from firm-to-firm in terms of whether it can be classified as value creation, depending on the firm's expertise and the relevance of the issue to the organization's vision and mission (and, therefore, to its stakeholders). *SVC* is not about activities peripheral to the firm, such as philanthropy; it is also not about redefining or reinventing capitalism; it is about the operational decisions the firm makes day-in and day-out (Principle 9). All aspects of business involve economic, social, moral, and ethical considerations and the primary role of the manager is to balance these considerations in prioritizing the diverse set of interests that have a stake in the firm's operations (Principle 1 and Principle 3).

The third component of *SVC* is that firms incorporate a stakeholder perspective throughout the firm. A barrier to the implementation of a stakeholder perspective, however, is the primary emphasis currently given by many corporations to the interests of its shareholders. Firms need to expand their view of stakeholders beyond shareholders (who neither own the firm, nor deserve any special attention from management and the Board), to include all of the firm's stakeholders who, collectively, define the firm's operating environment (Principle 2). In so doing, however, the firm has a responsibility not only to respond to stakeholder concerns, but also to anticipate these concerns whenever possible (Principle 3). For their part, stakeholders should be willing to enforce their needs onto firms by actively discriminating in favor of those firms that best meet expectations (Principle 4). By managing the firm in the interests of its broad range of stakeholders, the firm increases its chances of building a sustainable competitive advantage.

The fourth component of *SVC* relates to the drive to *optimize* (as opposed to *maximize*) value, broadly defined (Principle 6). In essence, the goal is to balance the production and consumption activities in society in order to build a standard of living that meets the needs of the collective (Principle 5). The production component includes incorporating costs that firms currently seek to externalize, while the consumption component includes incorporating costs that society currently seeks to avoid (Principle 7). If we can achieve this balance and spread both the benefits and the costs over a wide range of stakeholders, we will be significantly closer to optimizing value throughout society.

The final, and perhaps most important, component of *SVC* is the shift from a short-term perspective when managing the firm's resources and stakeholder relations to a medium- or long-term perspective. If managers alter their horizons from the next quarter or next season to the next decade or beyond, they immediately alter the priorities by which they manage and, as a result, automatically change the nature of the decisions they make today (Principle 2 and Principle 8). If a CEO is only interested in the next quarter, it is difficult to make the case for *SVC*. But, if the CEO is concerned with the continued existence of the firm 5, 10, or 20 years from now, the value of building lasting, trust-based relationships with key stakeholders increases exponentially.

These five components combine the ideas contained in the ten principles and define *SVC*. In short: Principle 1 identifies the for-profit firm as the most important organizational form in driving societal progress; Principle 2 locates stakeholder theory as central to operations; Principle 3 recognizes the practical importance for managers of being able to prioritize stakeholder interests; Principle 4 establishes the importance of stakeholders holding the firm to account; Principle 5 reminds us of the preeminent role of the market in producing optimal outcomes; Principle 6 notes that economic value and other kinds of value are not independent of each other; Principle 7 argues that, while the market is imperfect, it is more effective than all other organizing systems; Principle 8 highlights the importance of scale to achieving sustainability; Principle 9 states that all firms already create value, to varying degrees; and Principle 10 reaffirms the idea that business best serves society when it focuses on *business*, as illustrated by the previous nine principles.

Combining these ten principles, the five components of *SVC* are realized through a series of three conscious shifts that the firm's management team must make:

1   **Shift from the periphery to the core.** As indicated above, *SVC* is not about philanthropy; it is about core operations. As such, *SVC* must be applied to every major decision the firm takes. Culture is key, along

with leadership from the top. As long as the CEO understands that responding to stakeholder needs is central to the firm's ability to create value, then it immediately becomes central to what they do, every day.

2   **Shift from an externally oriented justification to an internally oriented justification.** The main value of *SVC* comes from its operational implications, not any reputational benefits. In particular, to internalize the ten principles of *SVC* is to understand that firms optimize value creation by responding to stakeholder needs. In terms of an organizing principle of the firm, all decisions made should be justified in terms of the value they create for stakeholders. If there is no value for anyone, the action should not be taken.

3   **Shift from short-term to long-term decision-making.** It matters intensely whether senior executives are building the firm for the long term versus aiming to meet analysts' quarterly projections. It is very difficult to justify *SVC* over the short term. Seeking to establish long-term, trust-based relations with all stakeholders, however, automatically changes the overriding priorities and the decisions the firm makes today. If the firm's executives change nothing else, they should aim to be "long-term greedy."[3]

Enlightened management

SVC delivers an operational and strategic advantage to the firm. As such, it is central to the goal of value creation, which is the primary purpose of the firm. In some ways, *SVC* is a subtle tweak of our economic model; in other ways, it is a radical transformation. It will increasingly become the most effective way for firms to create value in the business environment.

In essence, *SVC* represents an enlightened approach to management that retains the focus on adding value that is emphasized by a traditional bottom-line business model. Importantly, however, *SVC* incorporates a commitment to meet the needs and demands of the firm's broad range of stakeholder groups; it also recognizes the essential role stakeholders play in holding the firm to account for its actions. Equally important, in order to implement *SVC* comprehensively, the focus of the firm has to be on optimizing value over the long term by acting in areas in which it has expertise (related to core operations).

This focus on long-term added value is the principal difference between a traditional shareholder-focused business model and one based on *SVC* integrated throughout operations. This shift in perspective (from short to long term) is relatively easy to envision, but much more difficult to implement firm-wide. Nevertheless, this shift alone brings a firm significantly closer to building a competitive advantage that is truly sustainable. *SVC*, therefore, is as simple (and as complex) as conducting all aspects of business operations in a *responsible* manner – responding to those needs that stakeholders are willing to convey and enforce, with an emphasis on the medium to long term.

SVC focuses on evolution, not revolution, working within what we know about human psychology and economic exchange. As such, *SVC* encapsulates the way humans behave and business is conducted. It does not alter the goals of the firm (profit, except to say that a short-term focus is counter-productive) and it does not alter our understanding of fundamental economic theory (actors pursuing their self-interest can optimize value, broadly defined). What it does do, is alter the perspective from which operational and strategic decisions are made. For example, do the managers of the firm believe they can optimize performance by paying the firm's employees a *minimum* wage (because there is sufficient unemployment that, if one employee leaves, they can hire another one), or do the managers believe that they can optimize performance by paying the firm's employees a *living* wage (because it raises morale and productivity, while decreasing turnover rate and the hiring costs associated with replacing workers)? These two positions are substantively different approaches to business. Good arguments can be made in defense of both positions, but they are fundamentally different. This is the arena in which *SVC* operates. It is a progressive, enlightened approach to management that places the interests of a wide range of stakeholders within the decision matrix of the firm.[4]

The essential difference between those firms that do *SVC* well and those that do it badly, therefore, is a greater sensitivity to the needs and concerns of the firm's broad range of stakeholders. This provides the firm with an acute ability to understand when the (stakeholder-defined) rules that define the firm's operational context have changed, and a framework within which to apply that knowledge to the firm's strategic advantage. Those firms that can respond to (and, ideally, anticipate) those changes are better placed to survive and thrive in a dynamic business environment. Also, in striving to meet the needs and concerns of their stakeholders, those firms that engage in these activities in a more genuine, authentic way will find that the associated benefits are sustained because the effort is more effective and valued.

A short-term focus, driven by quarterly earnings guidance to investors with little long-term interest in the organization's survival, is of little concern (and is most likely detrimental) to firms committed to implementing *SVC*. Similarly, while economic value and other kinds of value (social, moral, ethical) cover similar ground, the overlap is not perfect. Externalities and transgressions are the result. Values help fill the gap and aid the *SVC* decision-making process.[5] To this end, a stakeholder filter is the tool the firm can use to apply its values to identify both potential opportunities and potential problems. The firm retains the societal legitimacy to remain an ongoing entity by seeking to implement its strategic plan and conduct operations while considering the needs and concerns of a broad array of stakeholders. The result is that, rather than profit *maximization* through a short-term focus, profit *optimization* emphasizes the importance of meeting the needs of these stakeholders over the medium to long term.

SVC, therefore, refines the economic system in which capitalism drives social and economic progress. The effects enhance the magnificent potential of business to alter our lives that has been summarized by some of the greatest business minds of our time:

> Profit for a company is like oxygen for a person. If you don't have enough of it, you're out of the game. But if you think your life is about breathing, you're really missing something.
>
> Peter Drucker[6]

> Being the richest man in the cemetery doesn't matter to me. ... Going to bed at night saying we've done something wonderful ... that's what matters to me.
>
> Steve Jobs[7]

In short, *SVC* equals value creation in today's complex and dynamic business environment – *sustainable* value creation. What does this mean in practice? Primarily, it means that those firms that "get" *SVC* will be able to create more value over a longer period of time than those firms that either do not understand the strategic value of this perspective, or ignore it altogether.

Final thoughts

As noted many years ago by Howard Bowen, the process of re-orienting capitalism to better suit the interests of society, broadly defined, is a complex process "which goes to the very root of our basic social and economic philosophy."[8] As a result, this task will not be achieved overnight. Given that we are working to reform a system that is already well-equipped to generate phenomenal economic and social progress, however, the task is also not unimaginable:

> The development of a moral code for business that can win wide acceptance and social sanction necessarily involves somewhat the same evolutionary process as characterizes the development of the law. ... We should not assume, however, that we are starting in this process from zero. Even under laissez faire, there was a system of moral rules for business.[9]

Much of what makes capitalism such a successful system already accommodates the complex web of norms, customs, and practices that are shaped by the values we share as a progressive, democratic society. Since Bowen wrote these words in 1953, these core moral values have been the source of a vast literature detailing the social responsibilities of corporations and the managers who run them. The concept of *SVC* is designed to contribute to this discussion and, hopefully, advance the debate toward the outcome that all those involved in the battle of ideas to improve our society wish to see.

——————— « » ———————

About the author

David Chandler (david.chandler@ucdenver.edu) is Associate Professor of Management at the University of Colorado Denver Business School. His research focuses on the dynamic interface between the firm and its institutional environment. This research has been published in *Administrative Science Quarterly, Academy of Management Journal, Organization Science, Academy of Management Review, Journal of Management,* and *Strategic Organization.* Additional related publications include the textbook *Strategic Corporate Social Responsibility: Sustainable Value Creation* (5e, Sage Publications, Inc., 2020). He received his Ph.D. in Management from The University of Texas at Austin in 2011.

Notes

Epigraph

1 Milton Friedman, *Capitalism and Freedom*, University of Chicago Press, 1962, Chapter VIII, p. 133.

Foreword

1 This Foreword appeared in the first edition of this book: David Chandler, *Corporate Social Responsibility: A Strategic Perspective*, Business Expert Press, 2015. Lynn Stout passed away in April 2018.

Introduction: Corporate Social Responsibility

1 Aneesh Raghunandan and Shiva Rajgopal, "Is There Real Virtue Behind the Business Roundtable's Signaling?" *The Wall Street Journal*, December 3, 2019, p. A15.
2 August 19, 2019, https://opportunity.businessroundtable.org/ourcommitment/
3 Klaus Schwab, "Davos Manifesto 2020: The Universal Purpose of a Company in the Fourth Industrial Revolution," *World Economic Forum*, December 2, 2019, www.weforum.org/agenda/2019/12/davos-manifesto-2020-the-universal-purpose-of-a-company-in-the-fourth-industrial-revolution/
4 The beginning of the modern CSR movement is often attributed either to Frank W. Abrams in 1951 ("Management's Responsibilities in a Complex World," *Harvard Business Review*, Vol. 29, Issue 3) or to Howard R. Bowen in 1953 (*Social Responsibilities of the Businessman*, Harper & Brothers).
5 Brad Plumer, "Carbon Dioxide Emissions Hit a Record in 2019, Even as Coal Fades," *The New York Times*, December 3, 2019, www.nytimes.com/2019/12/03/climate/carbon-dioxide-emissions.html
6 Milton Friedman, *Capitalism and Freedom*, University of Chicago Press, 1962, Chapter VIII, p. 133.
7 In his well-known 1970 *New York Times Magazine* article in which he declared CSR to be a "fundamentally subversive doctrine," Milton Friedman built part of his argument around the idea that "Only people can have responsibilities. ... 'business' as a whole cannot be said to have responsibilities." Putting aside the idea that a for-profit firm in our society can have *rights* (which Friedman recognizes and is not generally disputed) but not *responsibilities* (which Friedman dismisses and is disputed), in this book, the organization is the actor of primary focus. As such, I will refer to firms as entities that, for example, can "act in their own best interest." While I do not seek to anthropomorphize corporations, in order to discuss their

ability to create value it is necessary to separate the collective (the company) from the individuals who act on its behalf (executives, directors, and employees).

8 Christine Bader, "Why Corporations Fail to Do the Right Thing," *The Atlantic*, April 21, 2014, www.theatlantic.com/business/archive/2014/04/why-making-corporations-socially-responsible-is-so-darn-hard/360984/

9 Alexander Dahlsrud, "How Corporate Social Responsibility is Defined: An Analysis of 37 Definitions," *Corporate Social Responsibility and Environmental Management*, Vol. 15, 2008, p. 1.

10 Timothy M. Devinney, "Is the Socially Responsible Corporation a Myth? The Good, the Bad, and the Ugly of Corporate Social Responsibility," *Academy of Management Perspectives*, Vol. 23, 2009, p. 44.

11 See: Alexander Dahlsrud, "How Corporate Social Responsibility is Defined: An Analysis of 37 Definitions," *Corporate Social Responsibility and Environmental Management*, Vol. 15, 2008, pp. 1–13.

12 Mallen Baker, "PUMA Plucks Numbers Out of the CO2," May 17, 2011, www.mallenbaker.net/csr/post.php?id=394 (no longer available online).

13 The climate crisis has now reached the point where scientists believe we must declare a new geological age – the Anthropocene. This period is so-named because "humans, or rather, the industrial civilization they have created, have become the main factor driving the evolution of Earth." In: "Stopping a Scorcher," *The Economist*, November 23, 2013, p. 81. See also: Damian Carrington, "The Anthropocene Epoch: Scientists Declare Dawn of Human-influenced Age," *The Guardian*, August 29, 2016, www.theguardian.com/environment/2016/aug/29/declare-anthropocene-epoch-experts-urge-geological-congress-human-impact-earth

14 Fleming and Jones refer to CSR as the "opium of the people" for the intoxicating, but in their eyes misleading, prospect this idea holds for meaningful change within the current economic system. See: Peter Fleming and Marc T. Jones, *The End of Corporate Social Responsibility: Crisis & Critique*, Sage Publications, Inc., 2013, p. 67.

15 In December 2013, the American Customer Satisfaction Index released data correlating firms' customer service scores with their subsequent stock market performance, "suggesting that the most-hated companies perform better than their beloved peers. … there's no statistical relationship between customer-service scores and stock-market returns. … If anything, it might hurt company profits to spend money making customers happy." Quoted in: Eric Chemi, "Proof that it Pays to be America's Most-hated Companies," *Bloomberg*, December 17, 2013, www.bloomberg.com/news/articles/2013–12–17/proof-that-it-pays-to-be-americas-most-hated-companies

16 Timothy M. Devinney, "Is the Socially Responsible Corporation a Myth? The Good, the Bad, and the Ugly of Corporate Social Responsibility," *Academy of Management Perspectives*, Vol. 23, 2009, pp. 51, 52.

17 For examples of studies analyzing the relationship between CSR and firm performance, see Herman Aguinis and Ante Glavas, "What We Know and Don't Know About Corporate Social Responsibility: A Review and Research Agenda," *Journal of Management*, Vol. 38, Issue 4, 2012, pp. 932–968.

18 See the Sustainability Accounting Standards Board (www.sasb.org/), the Carbon Development Project (www.cdp.net/), and the Global Reporting Initiative (www.globalreporting.org/).

19 See "ESG 101: What is ESG Investing?" *MSCI*, www.msci.com/esg-investing/

20 "In the Thicket of It," *The Economist*, July 30, 2016, p. 52.

21 "On Purpose," *The Economist*, November 30, 2019, p. 59.

22 Alex Davidson, "What's a 'Good' Company, Anyway?" *The Wall Street Journal Report: Investing in Funds & ETFs*, April 4, 2016, p. R12.

23 James Mackintosh, "Social, Environmental Investment Scores Diverge," *The Wall Street Journal*, September 18, 2018, p. B10.

24 James Mackintosh, "Social, Environmental Investment Scores Diverge," *The Wall Street Journal*, September 18, 2018, p. B10.

25 The work Walmart (and other retailers) is doing to create a standardized "sustainability index" enabling comparisons of the ecological footprint across all its products carries the potential to revolutionize the way we measure social and environmental impact. See: The Sustainability Consortium: www.sustainability consortium.org/

26 See: Timothy M. Devinney, "Is the Socially Responsible Corporation a Myth? The Good, the Bad, and the Ugly of Corporate Social Responsibility," *Academy of Management Perspectives*, Vol. 23, 2009, pp. 44–56.

27 See: David Grayson and Adrian Hodges, "Corporate Social Opportunity! Seven Steps to Make Corporate Social Responsibility Work for Your Business," *Greenleaf Publishing*, July 2004.

28 F. Ernest Johnson, "Commentary on the Ethical Implications of the Study," in: Howard R. Bowen, *Social Responsibilities of the Businessman*, Harper & Brothers, 1953, p. 256.

29 "Subterranean Capitalist Blues," *The Economist*, October 26, 2013, p. 13.

30 Floyd Norris, "The Islands Treasured by Offshore Tax Avoiders," *The New York Times*, June 6, 2014, p. B1.

31 For insight into the futility of misaligned incentives that seek to subvert human nature, see: Steven Kerr, "On the Folly of Rewarding A, While Hoping for B," *Academy of Management Journal*, Vol. 18, No. 4, 1975, pp. 769–783.

32 See also: David Chandler (5th edition), *Strategic Corporate Social Responsibility: Sustainable Value Creation*, Sage Publications, Inc., 2020.

33 R. Edward Freeman, Jeffrey S. Harrison, Andrew C. Wicks, Bidhan L. Parmar, and Simone de Colle, *Stakeholder Theory: The State of the Art*, Cambridge University Press, 2010, p. 235.

34 R. Edward Freeman, Jeffrey S. Harrison, Andrew C. Wicks, Bidhan L. Parmar, and Simone de Colle, *Stakeholder Theory: The State of the Art*, Cambridge University Press, 2010, p. 235.

35 Howard R. Bowen, *Social Responsibilities of the Businessman*, Harper & Brothers, 1953, p. 52.

36 For a discussion on this issue, see: R. H. Coase, "The Problem of Social Cost," *Journal of Law and Economics*, Vol. 3, Issue 1, 1960, pp. 1–44.

37 For an understanding of this concept as originally constructed, see: Jean Jacques Rousseau, "The Social Contract: Or Principles of Political Right," public domain, 1762 (translated in 1782 by G. D. H. Cole).

Principle 1: Business is social progress

1 John Micklethwait and Adrian Wooldridge, *The Company: A Short History of a Revolutionary Idea*, The Modern Library, 2003, p. xx.

2 It is interesting to speculate about where organizations founded by social entrepreneurs fit within this taxonomy. The emergence of benefit corporations (and certified B Corps) further confuses traditional definitions of organizational forms. While CSR advocates often seek to place such organizations (which describe themselves as meeting social goals via business practices) as a hybrid that is best described as a "fourth type" of organization, my sense is they are no different from a for-profit. All companies exist to solve some social problem. In this sense, a supermarket is as much a *social enterprise* as TOMS Shoes; equally, they are both for-profit firms.

3 Jo Confino, "Interview: Unilever's Paul Polman on Diversity, Purpose and Profits," *The Guardian*, October 2, 2013, www.theguardian.com/sustainable-business/unilver-ceo-paul-polman-purpose-profits

4 Timothy M. Devinney, "Is the Socially Responsible Corporation a Myth? The Good, the Bad, and the Ugly of Corporate Social Responsibility," *Academy of Management Perspectives*, Vol. 23, 2009, p. 44.

5 John Micklethwait and Adrian Wooldridge, *The Company: A Short History of a Revolutionary Idea*, The Modern Library, 2003, p. xv.

6 Paul Polman, "Business, Society, and the Future of Capitalism," *McKinsey Quarterly*, Commentary, May 2014, www.mckinsey.com/business-functions/ sustainability/our-insights/business-society-and-the-future-of-capitalism

7 For more on this, see "Business as a Moral Endeavor," September 7, 2014, https://youtu.be/EseNAh9UwjI

8 Howard R. Bowen, *Social Responsibilities of the Businessman*, Harper & Brothers, 1953, p. 4.

9 Sally E. Blount, "Yes, the World Needs More MBAs. Here's Why," *Bloomberg*, May 13, 2014, www.bloomberg.com/news/articles/2014-05-13/yes-the-world-needs-more-mbas-dot-here-s-why

10 This debate is heavily influenced, of course, by the ultimate goal that the minimum wage seeks to achieve. Is its primary purpose to price labor (an economic function) or is it to reduce poverty (a social welfare function)? If the underlying goal is to reduce poverty, most economists agree that policies such as the earned income tax credit (a negative income tax for workers on low pay) is a much more effective means of achieving that outcome.

11 Walmart is often criticized for paying below market wage rates. In reality, however, the firm routinely receives applications that are many multiples the number of job openings available (which indicates above market wages). At the extreme, for example, in 2013, when the firm opened a store in Washington DC, it received more than 23,000 applications for the 600 positions it was advertising – an acceptance rate of 2.6% which, it was noted, is "more difficult than getting into Harvard [which] accepts 6.1% of applicants." In: Ashley Lutz, "Applicants for Jobs at the New DC Walmart Face Worse Odds than People Trying to Get into Harvard," *Business Insider*, November 19, 2013, www.businessinsider.com/ wal-mart-receives-23000-applications-2013-11

12 Bo Burlingham and George Gendron, "The Entrepreneur of the Decade: An Interview with Steven Jobs," *Inc.*, April 1, 1989, www.inc.com/magazine/ 19890401/5602.html

Principle 2: Shareholders do not own the firm

1 It is commonly understood that the original purpose of incorporation (by crown charter) was to accomplish continuity of life (beyond that of the original mix of an organization's investors). Limited liability was achieved over time by a legal sleight of hand, redrafting investor obligations in relation to calls for additional capital. If a bankrupt company had an enforceable right to call in capital from investors, for example to shore up the continued viability of an enterprise, creditors could claim that right as an asset of the firm and pursue the call (by right of subrogation). Gradually, lawyers began excluding these obligations, with the result that there was no legal claim for creditors to use, thus, by definition, limiting the investors' liability. Once established and accepted, limited liability gained its own legitimacy as an inducement to investors to support entrepreneurs in the value creation process.

2 Subhabrata Bobby Banerjee, "Corporate Social Responsibility: The Good, the Bad and the Ugly," *Critical Sociology*, Vol. 34, Issue 1, 2008, p. 53.

3 For a thorough discussion of the founding of the modern-day corporation and, in particular, the construction of the concept of limited liability, see: John

Micklethwait and Adrian Wooldridge, *The Company: A Short History of a Revolutionary Idea*, The Modern Library, 2003.

4 John Micklethwait and Adrian Wooldridge, *The Company: A Short History of a Revolutionary Idea*, Modern Library, 2003, pp. 43, 46.

5 It is important to note that this discussion relates primarily to the ownership and purpose of publicly traded corporations in the U.S. Although there are similarities, corporate law naturally varies across countries and cultures. And, even in the U.S., legal precedent governing firms differs among states, and whether they are private or closely held. This can be seen in *Revlon Inc. v. MacAndrews & Forbes Holdings, Inc.*, 506 A.2d 173 (Del. 1986), a case of limited application in which the Delaware Supreme Court announced, "where the company was being 'broken up' and shareholders were being forced to sell their interests in the firm to a private buyer, the board had a duty to maximize shareholder wealth by getting the highest possible price for the shares." See: Lynn A. Stout, "Why We Should Stop Teaching *Dodge v. Ford*," *Virginia Law & Business Review*, Vol. 3, No. 1, 2008, p. 172.

6 Martin Lipton and William Savitt, "The Many Myths of Lucian Bebchuk," *Virginia Law Review*, Vol. 93, Issue 3, 2007, p. 754.

7 "March of the Machines," *The Economist*, October 5, 2019, p. 19.

8 "Fast Times," *The Economist*, April 5, 2014, p. 73.

9 For a detailed exposition of how high-frequency traders utilize technology to exploit arbitrage opportunities in the market and trade on the intentions of other investors, see: Michael Lewis, *Flash Boys: A Wall Street Revolt*, W. W. Norton & Company, 2014. In essence: "High-frequency trading firms would post the 'best price' for every stock and then when hit with a trade, knowing there was a buyer in the market, take advantage of the fragmentation of exchanges and dark pools and latency (high-frequency traders can get to an exchange faster than you) to buy up shares from other HFTs or from Wall Street dark pools, and then nudge the price up and sell those shares. In other words, front run the customer. ... It's sleazy and maybe even illegal, akin to nanosecond-scale insider trading." In: Andy Kessler, "High-frequency Trading Needs One Quick Fix," *The Wall Street Journal*, June 16, 2014, p. A15.

10 "Fast Times," *The Economist*, April 5, 2014, p. 73.

11 "Stealth Socialism," *The Economist*, September 17, 2016, p. 73.

12 Rachel Evans, Sabrina Willmer, Nick Baker, and Brandon Kochkodin, "BlackRock and Vanguard Are Less Than a Decade Away from Managing $20 Trillion," *Bloomberg*, December 4, 2017, www.bloomberg.com/news/features/2017-12-04/blackrock-and-vanguard-s-20-trillion-future-is-closer-than-you-think

13 Robin Wigglesworth, "A Vast Money Machine Splutters," *Financial Times*, October 21/22, 2018, p. 9. While BlackRock is the largest asset manager in the world, Vanguard is "the largest U.S. provider of mutual funds and exchange-traded funds by assets and the second-largest money manager in the world." In: Sarah Krouse, "Vanguard 'Just Getting Started'," *The Wall Street Journal*, January 5, 2018, p. B1.

14 See John Authers and Chris Newlands, "Taking Over the Markets," *Financial Times*, December 6, 2016, p. 9.

15 John Maynard Keynes, *The General Theory of Employment, Interest and Money*, New York: Harcourt Brace and Co., 1936, p. 156.

16 Paul Krugman, "Now That's Rich," *The New York Times*, May 9, 2014, p. A25.

17 Howard R. Bowen, *Social Responsibilities of the Businessman*, Harper & Brothers, 1953, p. 34.

18 https://en.oxforddictionaries.com/ (accessed October 2018).

19 While a number of U.S. state corporate codes contain language that defines a *shareholder* as the owner of *shares*, which are "the units into which the proprietary interests in a corporation are divided" (e.g., Colorado Corporation Code, Section

7–101–401, clause 31), Delaware, "the single most important [U.S.] state for corporate law purposes … does not define the term stock or otherwise say what it represents. … The Delaware statute is simply silent on the issue of ownership." Julian Velasco, "Shareholder Ownership and Primacy," *University of Illinois Law Review*, Vol. 2010, No. 3, 2010, pp. 929–930. Due to this inconsistency in statutory law, it is fair to conclude that the essence of *ownership* lies in how corporate law is enforced (i.e., what it means in reality) and, in particular, how it is enforced in Delaware. In other words, how courts (particularly Delaware courts) interpret the relationship between corporations and shareholders, and apply that interpretation, is the ultimate determinant of who legally *owns* the corporation.

20 Luh Luh Lan and Loizos Heracleous, "Rethinking Agency Theory: The View from Law," *Academy of Management Review*, Vol. 35, No. 2, 2010, p. 301.

21 For related work that builds on the argument that the firm has obligations to its stakeholders, broadly defined, see: James E. Post, Lee E. Preston, and Sybille Sachs, *Redefining the Corporation: Stakeholder Management and Organizational Wealth*, Stanford Business Books, 2002 and Sybille Sachs and Edwin Ruhli's book, *Stakeholders Matter: A New Paradigm for Strategy in Society*, Cambridge University Press, 2012.

22 Martin Wolf, "AstraZeneca is More than Investors' Call,' *Financial Times*, May 8, 2014, www.ft.com/content/6fe31054-d691–11e3-b251–00144feabdc0

23 Eugene F. Fama, "Agency Problems and the Theory of the Firm," *Journal of Political Economy*, Vol. 88, 1980, p. 290.

24 Luh Luh Lan and Loizos Heracleous, "Rethinking Agency Theory: The View from Law," *Academy of Management Review*, Vol. 35, No. 2, 2010, p. 301.

25 "And what was particularly grotesque about this was that the Fourteenth amendment was passed to protect newly-freed slaves. So, for instance, between 1890 and 1910, there were 307 cases brought before the Court under the Fourteenth amendment – 288 of these brought by corporations; 19 by African-Americans. [As a result of the Civil War] 600,000 people were killed to get rights for people and then, with strokes of the pen over the next 30 years, judges applied those rights to capital and property, while stripping them from people." See: *The Corporation* documentary, 2003, www.thecorporation.com/

26 In reality, the detail of which rights and responsibilities should be legally ascribed to corporations and which should be reserved for humans alone is an ongoing constitutional debate. As a result, corporations are neither fully fledged individuals, nor are they artificial entities devoid of rights – legal precedent has determined they fall somewhere in-between: "In the past, Supreme Court opinions have recognized the need for differing approaches to the recognition (or not) of constitutional rights of business corporations in various settings. For example, the Court has decided that the constitutional protection against 'double jeopardy' for an alleged crime covers organizational persons (such as a corporation), but the right protecting against forcible 'self-incrimination' does not. Similarly, the Court has recognized a right of political free speech for organizations in *Citizens United*, but not 'rights to privacy' which have been reserved for individual human beings. In other words, the Court finds some constitutional rights make sense to extend to organizational persons, and it leaves others to cover only individual people." In: Eric W. Orts, "The 'Hobby Lobby' Case: Religious Freedom, Corporations and Individual Rights," *Knowledge@Wharton*, March 31, 2014, https://knowledge.wharton.upenn.edu/article/hobby-lobby-case-religious-freedom-corporations-individual-rights/

27 Jonathan R. Macey, "A Close Read of an Excellent Commentary on *Dodge v. Ford*," *Virginia Law & Business Review*, Vol. 3, No. 1, 2008, p. 180.

28 Jonathan R. Macey, "A Close Read of an Excellent Commentary on *Dodge v. Ford*," *Virginia Law & Business Review*, Vol. 3, No. 1, 2008, p. 190.

29 Joann S. Lublin and Theo Francis, "Where Majority Doesn't Rule," *The Wall Street Journal*, May 12, 2014, p. B8.

30 Joann S. Lublin and Theo Francis, "Where Majority Doesn't Rule," *The Wall Street Journal*, May 12, 2014, p. B8.

31 Joann S. Lublin and Theo Francis, "Where Majority Doesn't Rule," *The Wall Street Journal*, May 12, 2014, p. B8.

32 *HL Bolton (Engineering) v. TJ Graham and Sons Ltd.* [1957] 1 QB 159 (Court of Appeal), Denning LJ (p. 172).

33 Moreover, because investors are not one homogenous group with similar goals, investment timeframes, or values (they include pension funds, day-traders, and high-frequency computer algorithms), they cannot approximate the legal or actual influence of a sole proprietor who owns 100% of a firm's shares (or even a majority owner).

34 See: The Modern Corporation, "Statement on Company Law," clause 1, https://themoderncorporation.wordpress.com/company-law-memo/

35 For example, see: Jacob M. Rose, "Corporate Directors and Social Responsibility: Ethics versus Shareholder Value," *Journal of Business Ethics*, Vol. 73, Issue 3, July 2007, pp. 319–331. This study reports that "directors … sometimes make decisions that emphasize legal defensibility at the expense of personal ethics and social responsibility. Directors recognize the ethical and social implications of their decisions, but they believe that current corporate law requires them to pursue legal courses of action that maximize shareholder value" (p. 319).

36 In the business school, faculty are largely oblivious to this debate that is occurring in the academic corporate law community. For more information, see: https://themoderncorporation.wordpress.com/company-law-memo/

37 Julian Velasco, "Shareholder Ownership and Primacy," *University of Illinois Law Review*, Vol. 2010, No. 3, 2010, p. 899.

38 The corporate legal scholars who authored the statement, the "Fundamental rules of corporate law" at The Modern Corporation, https://themoderncorporation.wordpress.com/company-law-memo/, argue that this absence of a fiduciary responsibility of directors is "applicable in almost all jurisdictions."

39 For a detailed examination of the legal foundation (or lack of) for the idea that the primary fiduciary responsibility of the firm's executives and directors is to serve the interests of the firm's shareholders, see: Lynn Stout, *The Shareholder Value Myth: How Putting Shareholders First Harms Investors, Corporations, and the Public*. San Francisco, CA: Berrett-Koehler Publishers, Inc., 2012.

40 See: The Modern Corporation, "Fundamental Rules of Corporate Law," accessed in April, 2014, http://themoderncorporation.wordpress.com/company-law-memo/

41 Luh Luh Lan and Loizos Heracleous, "Rethinking Agency Theory: The View from Law," *Academy of Management Review*, Vol. 35, No. 2, 2010, p. 300.

42 *Dodge v. Ford Motor Company*, 204 Mich. 459, 170 N.W. 668 (1919).

43 Lynn A. Stout, "Why We Should Stop Teaching *Dodge v. Ford*," *Virginia Law & Business Review*, Vol. 3, No. 1, 2008, p. 166.

44 "*Dodge v. Ford* is best viewed as a case that deals not with directors' duties to maximize shareholder wealth, but with controlling shareholders' duties not to oppress minority shareholders. The one Delaware opinion that has cited *Dodge v. Ford* in the last 30 years, *Blackwell v. Nixon*, cites it for just this proposition." In: Lynn A. Stout, "Why We Should Stop Teaching *Dodge v. Ford*," *Virginia Law & Business Review*, Vol. 3, No. 1, 2008, p. 168.

45 Lynn A. Stout, "Why We Should Stop Teaching *Dodge v. Ford*," *Virginia Law & Business Review*, Vol. 3, No. 1, 2008, pp. 163–176.

46 An indirect attempt to rebut Stout's arguments was made by Leo E. Strine, Jr., Chief Justice of the Delaware Supreme Court, in an essay in the *Columbia Law Review* ("Can We Do Better by Ordinary Investors? A Pragmatic Reaction to the

Dueling Ideological Mythologists of Corporate Law," Vol. 114, Issue 2, pp. 449–502). The essay is primarily a response to the idea of the firm as a "shareholder-driven direct democracy" (p. 449), which advocates for wider shareholder powers and more frequent shareholder votes to govern firm policy. In arguing against this model, Strine also addresses the "skeptics [who] go so far as to deny that boards of directors must, within the constraints of the law, make the best interests of stockholders the end goal of the governance of a for-profit corporation" (p. 452). Unfortunately, however, Strine fails to acknowledge the near impossible task of defining what those "interests" might be (given that the firm's stockholders include high-frequency traders holding positions for microseconds, day-traders, and pension funds). He also bases his case on facts such as "only stockholders get to elect directors" (p. 453), as if that depicts ownership, without acknowledging that, in reality, shareholders vote on the candidates nominated by management and that additional *legal rights* are constrained because many votes (e.g., shareholder resolutions) are non-binding. Most damagingly, by undermining the idea of the direct democracy model (which would at least be more consistent with the idea of shareholders as owners) by arguing that "the best way to ensure that corporations generate wealth for diversified stockholders is to give the managers of corporations a strong hand to take risks and implement business strategies without constant disruption by shifting stock market sentiment," Strine essentially reinforces Stout's case that the Courts tend to favor management over stockholders in any dispute (the *business judgment rule*).

47 Lynn Stout, *The Shareholder Value Myth: How Putting Shareholders First Harms Investors, Corporations, and the Public*, Berrett-Koehler Publishers, Inc., San Francisco, CA, 2012, pp. 3–4.

48 Floyd Norris, "Companies That Lie Increasingly Win in Court," *The New York Times*, March 21, 2014, p. B1.

49 Loizos Heracleous and Luh Luh Lan, "The Myth of Shareholder Capitalism," *Harvard Business Review*, April, 2010, p. 24. See also: Luh Luh Lan and Loizos Heracleous, "Rethinking Agency Theory: The View from Law," *Academy of Management Review*, Vol. 35, No. 2, 2010, pp. 294–314.

50 Although, most of us are shareholders in that we are invested in pension funds; in reality, this relationship is indirect since these assets are managed by others on our behalf. Most people would not describe themselves primarily as a shareholder and, often, have a greater proportion of their total wealth invested in other assets, such as property.

51 It is important to draw a distinction between *rights* and *influence*. If executives believe shareholders own the firm, they will respond to their demands. This is true whether or not shareholders actually own the firm. It is interesting to ask, however, that: If shareholders have no legal power, how is this pressure manifested or felt, especially if the firm is not seeking additional capital? One answer highlights the extent to which executive compensation is increasingly tied to firm performance, which is often measured by share price. While this effect helps align the interests of executives and shareholders, it is not clear that the results benefit the long-term interests of the firm. See: Justin Fox and Jay W. Lorsch, "What Good Are Shareholders?" *Harvard Business Review*, July–August, 2012, pp. 49–57.

52 Danielle Chesebrough and Rory Sullivan, "What Can Companies Do about Investor Short-termism?' *Ethical Corporation Magazine*, November 26, 2013, www. ethicalcorp.com/stakeholder-engagement/what-can-companies-do-about-investor-short-termism

53 There are two ways that a firm can redistribute profits to its shareholders – share buybacks or dividends. While both methods ultimately raise the firm's share price, buybacks raise it directly (by decreasing the number of shares outstanding), while dividends do it indirectly (by making the shares a more attractive investment).

54 "Reform School for Bankers," *The Economist*, October 5, 2013, p. 73.
55 As noted by Robert Pozen of Harvard Business School, "At present, most firms distribute case bonuses and stock grants on the basis of the prior year's results. This approach does encourage top executives to favor short-term results over long-term growth." Robert C. Pozen, "The Misdirected War on Corporate Short-Termism," *The Wall Street Journal*, May 19, 2014, www.wsj.com/articles/robert-pozen-rx-for-corporate-short-termism-1400530829
56 Gregory J. Millman, "Firms See Value Opportunity in Shareholder Base," *The Wall Street Journal*, May 22, 2014, https://blogs.wsj.com/riskandcompliance/2014/05/22/the-morning-risk-report-companies-see-value-opportunity-in-shareholder-base/
57 Julian Velasco, "Shareholder Ownership and Primacy," *University of Illinois Law Review*, Vol. 2010, No. 3, 2010, pp. 901, 902.
58 In game theory, this concept of the likelihood of repeat or future interactions has been termed the "shadow of the future." See: Robert Axelrod, *The Evolution of Cooperation*, Basic Books, 1984.
59 An important step in the transition from shareholder to stakeholder focus is for the firm to prioritize its stakeholders (see Principle 3). In the process, firms should understand that a shareholder perspective and a stakeholder perspective are not alternatives. Although many commentators talk in terms of a choice between independent constructs; in reality, this is a forced dichotomy. Since shareholders are also stakeholders, a shareholder perspective is actually just a stakeholder perspective with a narrow focus on one stakeholder (shareholders) instead of many.
60 Joseph L. Bower and Lynn S. Paine, "The Error at the Heart of Corporate Leadership: Most CEOs and Boards Believe Their Main Duty is to Maximize Shareholder Value. It's Not," *Harvard Business Review*, May–June, 2017, p. 52.
61 See: State of Delaware General Corporation Law, https://delcode.delaware.gov/title8/c001/

Principle 3: Prioritizing competing stakeholder interests is difficult

1 R. Edward Freeman, *Strategic Management: A Stakeholder Approach*, Pitman, 1984, p. 46.
2 Frank W. Pierce, "Developing Tomorrow's Business Leaders," an address to the Cincinnati Chapter of the Society for the Advancement of Management, December 6, 1945, quoted in: Howard R. Bowen, *Social Responsibilities of the Businessman*, Harper & Brothers, 1953, p. 51.
3 Frank W. Abrams, "Management's Responsibilities in a Complex World," *Harvard Business Review*, Vol. 29, Issue 3, 1951, pp. 29, 30.
4 Howard R. Bowen, *Social Responsibilities of the Businessman*, Harper & Brothers, 1953, pp. 41–42.
5 Eric Rhenman, *Foeretagsdemokrati och foeretagsorganisation*, S.A.F. Norstedt: Företagsekonomiska Forsknings Institutet, Thule, Stockholm, 1964. See also: R. Edward Freeman, Jeffrey S. Harrison, Andrew C. Wicks, Bidhan L. Parmar, and Simone de Colle, *Stakeholder Theory: The State of the Art*, Cambridge University Press, 2010, p. 48.
6 R. Edward Freeman, *Strategic Management: A Stakeholder Approach*, Pitman, 1984, Chapter 2, pp. 31–51.
7 It is important to note that, while anyone who considers themselves a stakeholder can be thought of as such, the firm also plays an important role in identifying those stakeholders it considers important (as implied by the Freeman definition). In other words, it is conceivable that there are stakeholders who might not

consider themselves as such, but the company treats them as a stakeholder as a result of its operations or strategic interests.

8 It is interesting to debate whether the natural environment, as a non-independent actor, should be included as an identifiable stakeholder of the firm. Many argue that it should and that, in fact, the environment has rights that should be protected by law. Others, however, argue that it should not be included because it is not the environment itself that speaks or feels or acts; rather, it is how the degradation of the environment affects other stakeholder groups (e.g., NGOs or the government) who then advocate on its behalf. One argument for including the environment as one of the firm's societal stakeholders is to reinforce the importance of sustainability, while recognizing that the environment requires actors to speak and act on its behalf in order to be protected. For example, see: Jeremy Lurgio, "Saving the Whanganui: Can Personhood Rescue a River?" *The Guardian*, November 29, 2019, www.theguardian.com/world/2019/nov/30/saving-the-whanganui-can-personhood-rescue-a-river

9 For a network-based stakeholder perspective, see: James E. Post, Lee E. Preston, and Sybille Sachs, "Managing the Extended Enterprise: The New Stakeholder View," *California Management Review*, Vol. 45, Issue 1, 2002, pp. 6–28.

10 Howard R. Bowen, *Social Responsibilities of the Businessman*, Harper & Brothers, 1953, p. 102.

11 John Mackey, quoted in: April Fulton, "Whole Foods Founder John Mackey on Fascism and 'Conscious Capitalism'," *NPR*, January 16, 2013, www.npr.org/sections/thesalt/2013/01/16/169413848/whole-foods-founder-john-mackey-on-fascism-and-conscious-capitalism

12 John Mackey quoted in: John Bussey, "Are Companies Responsible for Creating Jobs?" *The Wall Street Journal*, October 28, 2011, p. B1.

13 Hedrick Smith, "When Capitalists Cared," *The New York Times*, September 2, 2012, www.nytimes.com/2012/09/03/opinion/henry-ford-when-capitalists-cared.html

14 Simon Zadek, "The Path to Corporate Responsibility," *Harvard Business Review*, December, 2004, pp. 125–132.

15 Simon Zadek, "The Path to Corporate Responsibility," *Harvard Business Review*, December, 2004, p. 127.

16 Simon Zadek, "The Path to Corporate Responsibility," *Harvard Business Review*, December, 2004, p. 128.

17 Jonah Sachs, "The Ultimate Missed Social-media Opportunity for Brands: Climate Change," *The Guardian*, March 12, 2014, www.theguardian.com/sustainable-business/social-marketing-brands-coke-chevrolet-climate-change-environment

18 An important contribution to this debate, for example, was made by Mitchell, Agle, and Wood's framework of "stakeholder salience," which helps greatly in identifying the stakeholders that, potentially, pose a threat to the firm (see: Ronald K. Mitchell, Bradley R. Agle, and Donna J. Wood, "Toward a Theory of Stakeholder Identification and Salience: Defining the Principle of Who and What Really Counts," *Academy of Management Review*, Vol. 22, Issue 4, 1997, pp. 853–886). Essentially, this model identifies the characteristics that render a stakeholder more or less salient to managers (power, legitimacy, and urgency). While important, stakeholder characteristics are only one of the factors that determine whether a firm should respond to a claim. Equally important are the characteristics of the firm (i.e., strategic relevance) and the characteristics of the issue (i.e., emerging or institutionalized). Mitchell et al. address these factors somewhat with their dimension of "urgency" (and also their idea of managers as a moderator of salience), but are not very specific about why or when something would be urgent. In reality, it is the intersection of all three factors (issue, stakeholder, and organization) that provides a clearer roadmap for managers as to when the firm

should act. More specifically, Mitchell et al. never really talk about prioritizing among competing interests. In other words, their model helps identify which stakeholders are important, but provides no real guidance as to which stakeholder the firm should support when interests conflict.

Principle 4: CSR is a stakeholder responsibility

1 For an extended discussion of this issue, see: T. M. Devinney, P. Auger, and G. M. Eckhardt, *The Myth of the Ethical Consumer*, Cambridge University Press, 2010.
2 For an example of the dangers associated with being too socially responsible, the story of Malden Mills and its Polartec line of clothing is instructive. See: Rebecca Leung, "The Mensch of Malden Mills," 60 Minutes, *CBS*, July 6, 2003, www.cbsnews.com/news/the-mensch-of-malden-mills/. See also, Gretchen Morgenson, "GE Capital vs. the Small-town Folk Hero," *The New York Times*, October 24, 2004, p. BU5.
3 The Merriam Webster dictionary, for example, defines the term *responsibility* as "moral, legal, or mental *accountability*," while the Oxford English Dictionary defines it as "the state or fact of being *accountable*" (emphasis added, see: www.merriam-webster.com/dictionary/ and www.oed.com/).
4 For a discussion on the cognitive constraints that limit stakeholders' ability or willingness to hold firms to account, see: Michael L. Barnett, "Why Stakeholders Ignore Firm Misconduct: A Cognitive View," *Journal of Management*, Vol. 40, Issue 3, 2014, pp. 676–702.
5 See also: David Chandler, "Why Aren't We Stressing Stakeholder Responsibility?" *Harvard Business Review Blog*, 2010, https://hbr.org/2010/04/why-arent-we-stressing-stakeho
6 Christine Bader, "Why Corporations Fail to Do the Right Thing," *The Atlantic*, April 21, 2014, www.theatlantic.com/business/archive/2014/04/why-making-corporations-socially-responsible-is-so-darn-hard/360984/
7 Howard R. Bowen, *Social Responsibilities of the Businessman*, Harper & Brothers, 1953, pp. 139–140.
8 Forest Reinhardt, Ramon Casadesus-Masanell, and Hyun Jin Kim, "Patagonia," *Harvard Business School*, October 19, 2010, [9–711–020], p. 8.
9 While a reasonable response to this statement is that the relationship between company and consumer is iterative (a sort of chicken and egg argument with an unclear origin), given that firms are less able to predict market trends than they are able to respond to those trends, it seems clear that the preeminent direction of influence is from consumer to company (and not the other way around).
10 Howard R. Bowen, *Social Responsibilities of the Businessman*, Harper & Brothers, 1953, p. 111.

Principle 5: Market-based solutions are optimal

1 Alice Korngold, "Business Can Do What Governments Can't: Solve the World's Biggest Problems," *The Guardian*, January 7, 2014, www.theguardian.com/sustainable-business/business-government-world-problems-davos-multinational
2 For an important historical and anthropological perspective on the role of the market as a medium for economic exchange (as well as possible alternatives), see: Karl Polanyi, *The Great Transformation: The Political and Economic Origins of Our Time*, Beacon Press, 1944.
3 Friedrich A. Hayek, *The Fatal Conceit: The Errors of Socialism*, Volume I of W. W. Bartley III (Ed.), *The Collected Works of Friedrich August Hayek*, Routledge, London, UK, 1988, p. 14.

4 John Authers, "Today's Liquid Markets Are Open to Hayekian Criticism," *Financial Times*, December 23, 2013, p. 12.

5 Alice Korngold, "Business Can Do What Governments Can't: Solve the World's Biggest Problems," *The Guardian*, January 7, 2014, www.theguardian.com/sustainable-business/business-government-world-problems-davos-multinational

6 Milton Friedman, interviewed on *The Donahue Show*, 1979, https://youtu.be/GapXLpLoZBs

7 Joseph E. Stiglitz, "Inequality Is Not Inevitable," *The New York Times*, June 29, 2014, p. SR7.

8 James Madison, "Federalist No. 51: The Structure of the Government Must Furnish the Proper Checks and Balances Between the Different Departments," February 6, 1788.

9 "A recent groundbreaking study found that undetected insider trading occurs in a stunning one-fourth of public-company deals." In: Editorial, "The Hidden Cost of Trading Stocks," *The New York Times*, June 23, 2014, p. A18.

10 For two excellent social psychology sources that discuss the bounded rationality of humans and the biases and heuristics that we apply in the absence of rationality, see: Herbert A. Simon, *Administrative Behavior: A Study of Decision-Making Processes in Administrative Organization*, The Free Press, 1976 and Daniel Kahneman, *Thinking, Fast and Slow*, Farrar, Straus and Giroux, 2011.

11 Quoted in: Steven Rattner, "Who's Right on the Stock Market?" *The New York Times*, November 15, 2013, p. A25.

12 Quoted in: Steven Rattner, "Who's Right on the Stock Market?" *The New York Times*, November 15, 2013, p. A25.

13 "Valuing the Long-beaked Echidna," *The Economist*, February 22, 2014, p. 66.

14 "Valuing the Long-beaked Echidna," *The Economist*, February 22, 2014, p. 66.

15 "The Colour of Pollution," *The Economist*, May 24, 2014, p. 29.

16 For a detailed consideration of the limits of federal government in the U.S., see: Peter H. Schuck, *Why Government Fails So Often*, Princeton University Press, 2014. For example, Schuck argues that, in order to be successful, "a public policy has to get six things right: incentives, instruments, information, adaptability, credibility and management. The federal government tends to be bad at all of these." And, where government intervention has proved to be most successful, it was generally because bureaucrats "did not try to manage success so much as establish the circumstances for it." In: Yuval Levin, "Open Door Policies," *The Wall Street Journal*, June 10, 2014, p. A13.

17 Howard R. Bowen, *Social Responsibilities of the Businessman*, Harper & Brothers, 1953, p. 26.

18 "The Logical Floor," *The Economist*, December 14, 2013, p. 18.

19 John Tierney, "When Energy Efficiency Sullies the Environment," *The New York Times*, March 8, 2011, p. D1.

20 John Tierney, "When Energy Efficiency Sullies the Environment," *The New York Times*, March 8, 2011, p. D1.

21 See: http://strategiccsr-sage.blogspot.com/2012/09/strategic-csr-prius-fallacy.html

22 For more on the human tendency to make rapid moral judgments and then rationalize them post hoc, see Jonathan Haidt, "The Emotional Dog and Its Rational Tail: A Social Intuitionist Approach to Moral Judgment," *Psychological Review*, Vol. 108, Issue No. 4, pp. 814–834, 2001.

23 John Tierney, "When Energy Efficiency Sullies the Environment," *The New York Times*, March 8, 2011, p. D1.

24 David Kestenbaum, "Pop Quiz: How Do You Stop Sea Captains from Killing Their Passengers?" *NPR*, September 10, 2010, www.npr.org/sections/money/2010/09/09/129757852/pop-quiz-how-do-you-stop-sea-captains-from-killing-their-passengers

25 Tomasz Obloj, "Financial Incentives and Bonus Schemes Can Spell Disaster for Business," *The Guardian*, December 11, 2013, www.theguardian.com/sustainable-business/financial-incentives-bonus-schemes-lloyds-fine

26 "Of Bongs and Bureaucrats," *The Economist*, January 11, 2014, p. 11.

27 "The Logical Floor," *The Economist*, December 14, 2013, p. 18.

28 David Sainsbury, "The Enabling State," *RSA Journal*, Spring, 2013, pp. 42–45, www.thersa.org/globalassets/pdfs/journals/spring-2013.pdf

29 Adam Smith, *The Wealth of Nations*, 1776, pp. 11–12.

30 Adam Gopnik, "Market Man," *The New Yorker*, October 18, 2010, Vol. 86, Issue 32, p. 82.

31 Daniel Kahneman, *Thinking, Fast and Slow*, Farrar, Straus and Giroux, New York, 2011.

32 Daniel Kahneman, *Thinking, Fast and Slow*, Farrar, Straus and Giroux, New York, 2011, pp. 411–412.

33 Richard H. Thaler and Cass R. Sunstein, *Nudge: Improving Decisions About Health, Wealth, and Happiness*, Penguin Books, 2009.

34 "Nudge, Nudge, Think, Think," *The Economist*, March 24, 2012, p. 78.

35 "Nudge, Nudge, Think, Think," *The Economist*, March 24, 2012, p. 78.

36 David Brooks, "The Unexamined Society," *The New York Times*, July 8, 2011, p. A21.

37 Brian Wansink, David R. Just, and Joe McKendry, "Lunch Line Redesign," *The New York Times*, October 22, 2010, p. 35.

38 Donald J. Boudreaux, "Thank You for Smoking," *The Wall Street Journal*, April 24, 2013, p. A13.

39 Richard H. Thaler and Cass R. Sunstein, *Nudge: Improving Decisions About Health, Wealth, and Happiness*, Penguin Books, 2009.

40 Donald J. Boudreaux, "Thank You for Smoking," *The Wall Street Journal*, April 24, 2013, p. A13.

41 Donald J. Boudreaux, "Thank You for Smoking," *The Wall Street Journal*, April 24, 2013, p. A13.

42 William C. Frederick, "The Growing Concern Over Business Responsibility," *California Management Review*, Vol. 2, Issue 4, 1960, p. 60.

43 N. Gregory Mankiw, "When the Scientist Is Also a Philosopher," *The New York Times*, March 23, 2014, p. BU4.

Principle 6: Profit = total value

1 Howard R. Bowen, *Social Responsibilities of the Businessman*, Harper & Brothers, 1953, p. 48.

2 Howard R. Bowen, *Social Responsibilities of the Businessman*, Harper & Brothers, 1953, p. 146.

3 Michael C. Jensen, "Value Maximization, Stakeholder Theory, and the Corporate Objective Function," *Business Ethics Quarterly*, Vol. 12, No. 2, 2002, p. 239.

4 Jennifer M. George, "Compassion and Capitalism: Implications for Organizational Studies," *Journal of Management*, Vol. 40, No. 1, January 2014, p. 5.

5 Edward Wyatt, "U.S. Struggles to Keep Pace in Delivering Broadband Service," *The New York Times*, December 30, 2013, p. B1.

6 Howard R. Bowen, *Social Responsibilities of the Businessman*, Harper & Brothers, 1953, p. 146.

7 Howard R. Bowen, *Social Responsibilities of the Businessman*, Harper & Brothers, 1953, pp. 89–90.

8 A control group is a separate group that undergoes the same experiment and is, essentially, exactly the same as the test group, apart from one variable (which is

the variable of interest to the researcher – in this case, it would be the policy or practice that the executive believes "maximizes" performance).

9 Robert Skidelsky, "4 Fallacies of Fiscal Austerity Debunked," *The Japan News by The Yomiuri Shimbun*, November 25, 2013, p. 9.
10 Howard R. Bowen, *Social Responsibilities of the Businessman*, Harper & Brothers, 1953, p. 114.
11 Michael C. Jensen, "Value Maximization, Stakeholder Theory, and the Corporate Objective Function," *Business Ethics Quarterly*, Vol. 12, No. 2, 2002, p. 245.

Principle 7: The *free* market is not free

1 "The Gated Globe," *The Economist*, October 12, 2013, p. 13.
2 Mitsuru Obe, "TPP Deal Expected to Shake Up Japan's Agriculture Sector," *The Wall Street Journal*, October 6, 2015, https://blogs.wsj.com/japanrealtime/2015/10/06/tpp-deal-expected-to-shake-up-japans-agriculture-sector/
3 "Scrap them," *The Economist*, June 14, 2014, p. 14.
4 Umair Irfan, "Fossil Fuels Are Underpriced by a Whopping $5.2 trillion," *Vox*, May 17, 2019, www.vox.com/2019/5/17/18624740/fossil-fuel-subsidies-climate-imf
5 While excessive government intervention usually undermines the market, an important exception is antitrust law, which is designed to prevent the consolidation of firms seeking monopolistic power. In the U.S. over the past several decades, therefore, it is the failure of government to intervene in multiple industries that has led to excessive concentration and a lack of competition. For example, "Americans have a choice between only two internet providers. The airline industry is dominated by four large carriers. Amazon, Apple, Facebook and Google are growing even larger. One or two hospital systems control many local markets. Home Depot and Lowe's have displaced local hardware stores. Regional pharmacy chains like Eckerd and Happy Harry's have been swallowed by national giants." In David Leonhardt, "Big Business Is Overcharging You," *The New York Times*, November 11, 2019, p. A23.
6 From 2009–2011, for example, the U.S. federal government "issued 106 new regulations," each of which is "expected to have an economic impact of at least $100m a year." See: 'Schumpeter, "Not Open for Business," *The Economist*, October 12, 2013, p. 78.
7 Michael J. Ybarra, "Free to Choose, and Conserve," *The Wall Street Journal*, June 11, 2012, p. A11.
8 Adam Smith published *The Wealth of Nations* in 1776, but it is his book, *The Theory of Moral Sentiments* (first published in 1759), that leads many observers to describe Smith as a moral philosopher, rather than an economist. For example, see: James R. Otteson, "Adam Smith: Moral Philosopher," *Foundation for Economic Education*, November 1, 2000, https://fee.org/articles/adam-smith-moral-philosopher/
9 Nathan M. Jensen, "Do Taxpayers Know They Are Handing Out Billions to Corporations?" *The New York Times*, April 24, 2018, www.nytimes.com/2018/04/24/opinion/amazon-hq2-incentives-taxes.html
10 Paul Krugman, "Here Comes the Sun," *The New York Times*, November 7, 2011, p. A21.
11 Paul Krugman, "Here Comes the Sun," *The New York Times*, November 7, 2011, p. A21.
12 Gernot Wagner, "Going Green but Getting Nowhere," *The New York Times*, September 8, 2011, p. A25.
13 John Maynard Keynes, *A Tract on Monetary Reform*, Macmillan Publishers, 1923, pp. 79–80.

14 Al Gore and David Blood, "For People and Planet," *The Wall Street Journal*, March 28, 2006, p. A20.
15 Jason Clay, "How Big Brands Can Save Biodiversity," *TEDGlobal 2010*, July, 2010, www.ted.com/talks/jason_clay_how_big_brands_can_help_save_biodiversity
16 See Elien Blue Becque, "Elon Musk Wants to Die on Mars," *Vanity Fair*, March 10, 2013, www.vanityfair.com/news/tech/2013/03/elon-musk-die-mars
17 Nathaniel Rich, "Earth Control," *The New York Times Book Review*, October 13, 2013, p. 18.
18 Charles Eisenstein, "Concern About Overpopulation is a Red Herring; Consumption's the Problem," *The Guardian*, March 28, 2014, www.theguardian.com/sustainable-business/blog/concern-overpopulation-red-herring-consumption-problem-sustainability
19 For more information on how humans are the only species that creates "toxic waste," see: Paul Hawken, *The Ecology of Commerce: A Declaration of Sustainability*, HarperCollins Publishers, 1993.
20 The advances made by firms such as Interface Carpets demonstrate the efficiencies that are open to firms that understand *waste* as a commodity, rather than a cost. See: www.interface.com/SEA/en-SEA/sustainability/our-journey-en
21 Paul Hawken, *The Ecology of Commerce: A Declaration of Sustainability*, HarperCollins Publishers, 1993, p. 13.
22 A related concept to lifecycle pricing is the *circular economy*. While lifecycle pricing focuses on ensuring all costs of production and consumption are included in the price charged for a product, the circular economy focuses on eradicating waste by improving the design of products to either be easily repaired, re-used, or recycled. For more information, see: www.theguardian.com/sustainable-business/series/circular-economy
23 A Pigovian tax is an instrument designed to remedy a market imperfection by taxing a behavior that generates third-party costs (i.e., an externality) that are otherwise unaccounted for in the market price for the product, such as a carbon tax. For more information about Pigovian taxes, see: R. H. Coase, "The Problem of Social Cost," *The Journal of Law & Economics*, Vol. III, October 1960, pp. 1–44 and William J. Baumol, "On Taxation and the Control of Externalities," *The American Economic Review*, Vol. 62, June 1972, pp. 307–322.
24 For an early discussion of the challenges inherent in adopting a lifecycle management program within the firm, see: Mark Sharfman, Rex T. Ellington, and Mark Meo, "The Next Step in Becoming 'Green': Life-cycle Oriented Environmental Management," *Business Horizons*, May–June, 1997, pp. 13–22.
25 Andrew Martin, "How Green Is My Orange?" *The New York Times*, January 21, 2009, www.nytimes.com/2009/01/22/business/22pepsi.html
26 Usman Hayat, "Future Challenges for Sustainable Investing," *Financial Times (FTfm)*, February 7, 2011, p. 12.
27 Marc Gunther, "Natural Capital: Breakthrough or Buzzword?" *The Guardian*, March 6, 2014, www.theguardian.com/sustainable-business/natural-capital-nature-conservancy-trucost-dow
28 Sissel Waage, "How Can the Value of Nature Be Embedded in the World of Business?" *The Guardian*, March 31, 2014, www.theguardian.com/sustainable-business/finance-nature-no-value-natural-capital
29 "PUMA Completes First Environmental Profit and Loss Account which values Impacts at €145 million," *PUMA*, November 16, 2011, https://about.puma.com/en/newsroom/corporate-news/2011/11-16-11-first-environmental-profit-and-loss. See also: Richard Anderson, "Puma First to Publish Environmental Impact," *BBC News*, May 16, 2011, www.bbc.co.uk/news/business-13410397
30 Andrew Ward, "Exxon Backs *Serious* Climate Change Action," *Financial Times*, October 20, 2016, p. 16.

31 "Low-carb Diet," *The Economist*, January 13, 2018, p. 58.

32 "Low-carb Diet," *The Economist*, January 13, 2018, p. 58.

33 See: "Ray Anderson: Mount Sustainability," *WatchMojo.com*, October 8, 2009, https://youtu.be/l_P_V0jk3Ig

34 Ray Anderson, "The Business Logic of Sustainability," *TED2009*, February, 2009, www.ted.com/talks/ray_anderson_the_business_logic_of_sustainability

35 While the CSR community has done a reasonable job of holding firms responsible for their supply chain, the group seems less willing to apply the same standards to firms further up the distribution chain. Why are extraction firms, for example, not held accountable for subsequent uses of the raw materials they take out of the ground? While there has been some discussion of *conflict diamonds/minerals*, responsibility for the supply chain appears to rest with the firm that sells the finished product, rather than the firm that sold the raw materials or component parts. This is an issue that has yet to emerge for distributors, but it is not difficult to imagine a day when that happens. Rather than hold GAP, Nike, and Walmart responsible for the actions of other firms far removed from them closer to source, it surely makes more sense to hold the extraction firms themselves responsible for their own actions.

36 For a discussion about the limits of our current economic model based around growth and consumption, see: Tim Jackson, "New Economic Model Needed Not Relentless Consumer Demand,' *The Guardian*, January 18, 2013, www.the guardian.com/sustainable-business/blog/new-economic-model-not-consumer-demand-capitalism

Principle 8: Only business can save the planet

1 For a more detailed discussion of the environmental consequences of an expanding population and a static resource base, see: Garrett Hardin, "Tragedy of the Commons," *Science*, Vol. 162, No. 3859, December 13, 1968, pp. 1243–1248, https://science.sciencemag.org/content/162/3859/1243.full

2 Michael Pollan, "Why Bother?" *The New York Times*, April 20, 2008, p. 19.

3 Brad Plumer, "Carbon Dioxide Emissions Hit a Record in 2019, Even as Coal Fades," *The New York Times*, December 3, 2019, www.nytimes.com/2019/12/03/climate/carbon-dioxide-emissions.html

4 Paul Hawken, *The Ecology of Commerce: A Declaration of Sustainability*, Harper-Collins, 1993, pp. 4, 5.

5 "Our Common Future, Chapter 2: Towards Sustainable Development," *UN Documents*, www.un-documents.net/ocf-02.htm

6 In defining the term *sustainability*, it is useful to distinguish between the use of *sustainability* as a noun and *sustainable* as an adjective. Although, grammatically, the two words clearly share the same etymology; in practical terms, there is a difference. In most uses of the term *sustainability*, such as by the media, for example, the intended reference is almost always to the environment. When *sustainable* is being used to qualify the word *business*, however (i.e., a *sustainable* business; a term that can be used interchangeably with *Sustainable Value Creation*), the meaning conveyed is closer to the original, broad meaning of a business that is self-sustaining.

7 In the U.S., for example, when survey respondents were asked what words they most closely associate with *sustainability*, the most common responses were "'environmentally friendly,' 'natural,' 'organic,' 'green,' 'recycle' and 'renewable.' … Meanwhile, words such as 'ethical,' 'trust,' 'trustworthy,' 'collaboration,' community' and 'transparency' ranked low in their perceived relationship to sustainability." See: "Open Thread: What Does 'Sustainable' Mean to You?" *The Guardian*, February 3, 2014, www.theguardian.com/sustainable-business/sustainable-green-meaning-consumer-open-thread

8 Bill Baue, "Brundtland Report Celebrates 20th Anniversary Since Coining Sustainable Development," *Social Funds*, June 11, 2007, www.socialfunds.com/news/article.cgi/article2308.html (no longer online).

9 Nathaniel Rich, "Losing Earth: The Decade We Almost Stopped Climate Change," *The New York Times Magazine*, August 5, 2018, www.nytimes.com/interactive/2018/08/01/magazine/climate-change-losing-earth.html

10 "Global Greenhouse Gas Emissions Data," *U.S. Environmental Protection Agency*, January, 2020, www.epa.gov/ghgemissions/global-greenhouse-gas-emissions-data

11 Danielle Wiener-Bronner, "Forget Plastic Straws, Starbucks Has a Cup Problem," *CNN Business*, February 27, 2019, https://edition.cnn.com/interactive/2019/02/business/starbucks-cup-problem/index.html

12 "Made to Break: Are we Sinking under the Weight of our Disposable Society?" *Knowledge@Wharton*, August 9, 2006, https://knowledge.wharton.upenn.edu/article/made-to-break-are-we-sinking-under-the-weight-of-our-disposable-society/

13 "Talking Trash," *The Economist Technology Quarterly*, June 2, 2012, p. 12. See also: 'Municipal Waste,' *OECD Data*, https://data.oecd.org/waste/municipal-waste.htm

14 Brook Larmer, "The World's Fastest-growing Trash Stream, e-Waste, Offers Economic Opportunity as Well as Toxicity," *The New York Times Magazine*, July 8, 2018, p. 12.

15 Brook Larmer, "The World's Fastest-growing Trash Stream, e-Waste, Offers Economic Opportunity as Well as Toxicity," *The New York Times Magazine*, July 8, 2018, p. 12.

16 Annie Leonard, "Our Plastic Pollution Crisis is Too Big for Recycling to Fix," *The Guardian*, June 9, 2018, www.theguardian.com/commentisfree/2018/jun/09/recycling-plastic-crisis-oceans-pollution-corporate-responsibility

17 Lucy Siegle, "Yes, Plastic is an Eco Nightmare. But it's Also Tired, Old Technology," *The Guardian*, July 21, 2018, www.theguardian.com/commentisfree/2018/jul/21/yes-plastic-is-an-eco-nightmare-but-its-also-tired-old-technology

18 Mike Ives, "On Thai Beach, Grim Symbol of the Rise in Plastic Pollution," *The New York Times*, June 5, 2018, p. A4.

19 Joseph Curtin, "Let's Bag Plastic Bags," *The New York Times*, March 4, 2018, p. SR10.

20 Lee Scott, "Twenty First Century Leadership," October 23, 2005, https://corporate.walmart.com/_news_/executive-viewpoints/twenty-first-century-leadership

21 Lee Scott, "Twenty First Century Leadership," October 23, 2005, https://corporate.walmart.com/_news_/executive-viewpoints/twenty-first-century-leadership

22 See https://corporate.walmart.com/our-story/our-business

23 "Wal-Mart Completes Goal to Sell Only Concentrated Liquid Laundry Detergent," May 29, 2008, https://corporate.walmart.com/newsroom/2008/05/29/wal-mart-completes-goal-to-sell-only-concentrated-liquid-laundry-detergent

24 For more detail, see the Sustainability Consortium (www.sustainabilityconsortium.org/) and Walmart's webpage on the Sustainability Index, www.walmartsustainabilityhub.com/sustainability-index

25 As individuals, companies, and nation states, our massive levels of debt continue to threaten our economic stability. For example, see William D. Cohan, "The Debt Crisis Is Coming," *The New York Times*, September 1, 2019, p. SR2.

26 Avis Cardella, "Attention, Shoppers," *The New York Times Book Review*, February 10, 2013, p. 21.

27 Avis Cardella, "Attention, Shoppers," *The New York Times Book Review*, February 10, 2013, p. 21.

28 Avis Cardella, "Attention, Shoppers," *The New York Times Book Review*, February 10, 2013, p. 21.

29 See: T. M. Devinney, P. Auger, and G. M. Eckhardt, *The Myth of the Ethical Consumer*, Cambridge University Press, 2010. Also, this effect is enhanced when

action involves *change* because humans instinctively value the status quo and fear the unknown: "According to a study of referendums worldwide, voters almost always reject change: if the campaign starts with opinion evenly balanced, the status quo wins in 80 per cent of cases." Rachel Sylvester, "Voters Always Know Best, That's Why it Pays Not to Ask Them," *The Times* in *The Daily Yomiuri*, October 21, 2012, p. 8.

30 Katherine White, David J. Hardisty, and Rishad Habib, "The Elusive Green Consumer,' *Harvard Business Review*, July/August, 2019, https://hbr.org/2019/07/the-elusive-green-consumer

31 For example: "Pound for pound, making a Prius contributes more carbon to the atmosphere than making a Hummer, largely due to the environmental cost of the 30 pounds of nickel in the hybrid's battery. ... If a new Prius were placed head-to-head with a used car, would the Prius win? Don't bet on it. Making a Prius consumes 113 million BTUs. ... A single gallon of gas contains about 113,000 Btus, so Toyota's green wonder guzzles the equivalent of 1,000 gallons before it clocks its first mile. A used car, on the other hand, starts with a significant advantage: The first owner has already paid off its carbon debt. Buy a decade-old Toyota Tercel, which gets a respectable 35 mpg, and the Prius will have to drive 100,000 miles to catch up." In: "Inconvenient Truths: Get Ready to Rethink What It Means to Be Green," *Wired*, May 19, 2008, www.wired.com/2008/05/ff-heresies-intro/

32 Joseph Rago, "Conspicuous Virtue and the Sustainable Sofa," *The Wall Street Journal*, March 23, 2007, p. W13.

33 Joseph Rago, "Conspicuous Virtue and the Sustainable Sofa," *The Wall Street Journal*, March 23, 2007, p. W13.

34 See: Wesley Morris, "Tie a Yellow Bracelet," *Grantland*, August 28, 2012, https://grantland.com/features/livestrong-founder-lance-armstrong-was-never-really-cycling/

35 Joseph Rago, "Conspicuous Virtue and the Sustainable Sofa," *The Wall Street Journal*, March 23, 2007, p. W13.

36 In April 2010, an oil well owned by Transocean and operated by BP (with support from Halliburton) exploded killing 11 men and releasing "approximately 168 million gallons of oil in the Gulf of Mexico." In "Oil Spills Fast Facts," *CNN Library*, April 22, 2019, https://edition.cnn.com/2013/07/13/world/oil-spills-fast-facts/index.html

37 NOAA, "Gulf of Mexico 'Dead Zone' Predictions Feature Uncertainty," *ScienceDaily*, June 21, 2012, www.sciencedaily.com/releases/2012/06/120621113419.htm

38 The Cuyahoga River in Ohio is famous for catching fire numerous times in the 1950s and 1960s. The river was the focus of a 1969 *Time Magazine* report about the levels of pollution in many U.S. rivers, being described as a river that "oozes, rather than flows." The report prompted public outrage and helped build support for the nascent environmental movement. One outcome was the establishment of the Environmental Protection Agency (a U.S. federal government agency) by President Richard Nixon in 1970. See "America's Sewage System and the Price of Optimism," *Time Magazine*, August 1, 1969, http://content.time.com/time/magazine/article/0,9171,901182,00.html

39 "Stopping a Scorcher," *The Economist*, November 23, 2013, p. 80.

40 Adam Corner, "'Every Little Helps' Is a Dangerous Mantra for Climate Change," *The Guardian*, December 13, 2013, www.theguardian.com/sustainable-business/plastic-bags-climate-change-every-little-helps

41 Adam Corner, "'Every Little Helps' Is a Dangerous Mantra for Climate Change," *The Guardian*, December 13, 2013, www.theguardian.com/sustainable-business/plastic-bags-climate-change-every-little-helps

42 Howard R. Bowen, *Social Responsibilities of the Businessman*, Harper & Brothers, 1953, p. 227.
43 For background about this report, see *Stern Review on the Economics of Climate Change*, HM Treasury, 2006, https://webarchive.nationalarchives.gov.uk/+tf_/www.hm-treasury.gov.uk/sternreview_index.htm
44 John Kay, "Climate Change: The (Groucho) Marxist Approach," *Financial Times*, November 28, 2007, p. 11.
45 John Kay, "Climate Change: The (Groucho) Marxist Approach," *Financial Times*, November 28, 2007, p. 11.
46 Marc Gunther, "Sustainability at McDonald's. Really," September 24, 2013, www.marcgunther.com/sustainability-at-mcdonalds-really/ (no longer available online). See also: Marc Gunther, "Coffee and the Consumer: Can McDonald's Mainstream Sustainability?" *The Guardian*, September 24, 2013, www.theguardian.com/sustainable-business/mcdonalds-coffee-sustainability
47 Livia Albeck-Ripka, "Your Recycling Gets Recycled, Right? Maybe, or Maybe Not," *The New York Times*, May 29, 2018, www.nytimes.com/2018/05/29/climate/recycling-landfills-plastic-papers.html
48 Erica Grieder, "One Man's Trash Is Another's Trade," *The Wall Street Journal*, December 21–22, 2013, p. C9.
49 Luca Ventura, "World's Largest Companies 2019," *Global Finance Magazine*, August 29, 2019, www.gfmag.com/global-data/economic-data/largest-companies
50 Jason Clay, "How Big Brands Can Save Biodiversity," *TEDGlobal 2010*, July, 2010, www.ted.com/talks/jason_clay_how_big_brands_can_help_save_biodiversity

Principle 9: Value creation is not a choice

1 Paul C. Godfrey, "The Relationship between Corporate Philanthropy and Shareholder Wealth: A Risk Management Perspective," *Academy of Management Review*, Vol. 30, Issue 4, 2005, pp. 777–798.
2 Paul Sullivan, "Firms Learn as They Help Charities, They Also Help Their Brands," *The New York Times*, November 6, 2017, www.nytimes.com/2017/11/06/business/corporate-philanthropy.html
3 Graham McLaughlin, "Why Brands Should Focus on Social Change, Not Philanthropy," *The Guardian*, January 17, 2014, www.theguardian.com/sustainable-business/responsibility-good-business-long-term
4 "The Ultimate List of Charitable Giving Statistics for 2018," *Nonprofit Source*, https://nonprofitssource.com/online-giving-statistics/
5 Warren A. Stephens, "Why Do the Young Reject Capitalism?" *The Wall Street Journal*, June 1, 2017, p. A17. More specifically, "A Recent YouGov Poll Found that the Share of 18-to-29 Year Olds with a Favorable View of Capitalism Slipped to 30% in 2018 from 39% in 2015," in Edward Glaeser, "The Commercial Republic," *The Wall Street Journal*, October 20–21, 2018, p. C9.
6 Mark Boleat, "Inclusive Capitalism: Searching for a Purpose beyond Profit," *The Guardian*, May 27, 2014, www.theguardian.com/sustainable-business/inclusive-capitalism-purpose-beyond-profit
7 In this sense, the work of C. K. Prahalad and Stuart Hart on delivering goods and services to consumers at the bottom-of-the-pyramid is instructive because the conceptualization of the developing world as an under-served market (rather than a charitable cause) speaks to the power of business to deliver market-based solutions that address some of society's most intractable problems. See: C. K. Prahalad, *The Fortune at the Bottom of the Pyramid: Eradicating Poverty Through Profits*, Wharton School Publishing, 2004 and Stuart L. Hart, *Capitalism at the Crossroads: The*

Unlimited Business Opportunities in Solving the World's Most Difficult Problems, Wharton School Publishing, 2005.

8 A transcript of Gates' remarks, together with a link to a video of his January 24, 2008 speech, can be found at: www.gatesfoundation.org/media-center/speeches/2008/01/bill-gates-2008-world-economic-forum

9 A transcript of Gates' remarks, together with a link to a video of his January 24, 2008 speech, can be found at: www.gatesfoundation.org/media-center/speeches/2008/01/bill-gates-2008-world-economic-forum

10 Michael Kanellos, "On 'Creative Capitalism,' Gates Gets It," *CNET*, January 25, 2008, www.cnet.com/news/on-creative-capitalism-gates-gets-it/

11 Declan McCullagh, "Gates Misses the Point On 'Creative Capitalism'," *CNET*, January 25, 2008, www.cnet.com/news/gates-misses-the-point-on-creative-capitalism/

12 William R. Easterly, "Why Bill Gates Hates My Book," *The Wall Street Journal*, February 7, 2008, p. A18.

13 See: Muhammad Yunus, *Creating a World Without Poverty: Social Business and the Future of Capitalism*, Public Affairs, 2008.

14 Alan Beattie, "Poor Returns," *Financial Times*, February 2, 2008, p. 33.

15 Alan Beattie, "Poor Returns," *Financial Times*, February 2, 2008, p. 33.

16 Michael E. Porter and Mark R. Kramer, "Creating Shared Value," *Harvard Business Review*, 2011, Vol. 89, p. 64.

17 For additional commentary on Porter and Kramer's ideas, see: Tobias Webb, "Does Michael Porter Understand Sustainable Business?" January 21, 2011, http://sustainablesmartbusiness.com/does-michael-porter-understand/

18 Andrew Hill, "Society and the Right Kind of Capitalism," *Financial Times*, February 22, 2011, p. 14.

19 See: William B. Werther and David Chandler, "Strategic Corporate Social Responsibility as Global Brand Insurance," *Business Horizons*, Vol. 48, issue 4, 2005, pp. 317–324.

Principle 10: The *business* of business is business

1 Milton Friedman, "The Social Responsibility of Business is to Increase its Profits," *The New York Times Magazine*, September 13, 1970, www.nytimes.com/1970/09/13/archives/a-friedman-doctrine-the-social-responsibility-of-business-is-to.html

2 Jo Confino, "Interview: Unilever's Paul Polman on Diversity, Purpose and Profits," *The Guardian*, October 2, 2013, www.theguardian.com/sustainable-business/unilver-ceo-paul-polman-purpose-profits

3 Milton Friedman, "The Social Responsibility of Business is to Increase its Profits," *The New York Times Magazine*, September 13, 1970, www.nytimes.com/1970/09/13/archives/a-friedman-doctrine-the-social-responsibility-of-business-is-to.html

4 Milton Friedman, "The Social Responsibility of Business is to Increase its Profits," *The New York Times Magazine*, September 13, 1970, www.nytimes.com/1970/09/13/archives/a-friedman-doctrine-the-social-responsibility-of-business-is-to.html

5 Charles Handy, "What's a Business For?" *Harvard Business Review*, December, 2002, pp. 49–55.

6 Charles Handy, "What's a Business For?" *Harvard Business Review*, December, 2002, p. 52.

7 Milton Friedman, "The Social Responsibility of Business is to Increase its Profits," *The New York Times Magazine*, September 13, 1970, www.nytimes.com/1970/09/13/archives/a-friedman-doctrine-the-social-responsibility-of-business-is-to.html

8 Milton Friedman, "The Social Responsibility of Business is to Increase its Profits," *The New York Times Magazine*, September 13, 1970, www.nytimes.com/1970/09/13/archives/a-friedman-doctrine-the-social-responsibility-of-business-is-to.html

9 Archie B. Carroll, "The Pyramid of Corporate Social Responsibility: Toward the Moral Management of Organizational Stakeholders," *Business Horizons*, July–August, 1991, p. 43.

Conclusion: Sustainable Value Creation

1 See also: David Chandler (5th edition), *Strategic Corporate Social Responsibility: Sustainable Value Creation*, Sage Publications, Inc., 2020.

2 If there was one single change I would make to implement the ideas contained in this book in any publicly traded firm, it would be to change the existing *Investor Relations Department* into a *Stakeholder Relations Department* with the expanded mandate this title implies.

3 "Reform School for Bankers," *The Economist*, October 5, 2013, p. 73.

4 For additional discussion around the idea that *SVC* represents progressive management, see: Thomas E. Graedel and Braden R. Allenby, *Industrial Ecology and Sustainable Engineering*, Prentice Hall, 2009. The authors are industrial ecologists who argue that there is no such thing as *green management*, only *good management*.

5 Firms that understand the powerful motivating force of a values-based business include Zappos, Nike, Whole Foods, and Patagonia. Inspiring people, however, is difficult and expensive. As such, it appears most firms prefer a thin veil of values to bolster their compliance and avoid alienating anyone (a neutral approach). The difference is between firms that understand the powerful and radical consequences of implementing *SVC* and those that do not.

6 Innovation & Design, "Peter Senge's Necessary Revolution," *Bloomberg*, June 11, 2008, www.bloomberg.com/news/articles/2008–06–11/peter-senges-necessary-revolutionbusinessweek-business-news-stock-market-and-financial-advice

7 G. Pascal Zachary and Ken Yamada, "What's Next? Steve Job's Vision, So on Target at Apple, Now Is Falling Short," *The Wall Street Journal*, May 25, 1993, www.wsj.com/articles/SB10001424052970203476804576614371332161748

8 Howard R. Bowen, *Social Responsibilities of the Businessman*, Harper & Brothers, 1953, p. 228.

9 Howard R. Bowen, *Social Responsibilities of the Businessman*, Harper & Brothers, 1953, p. 193.